P9-CMB-227

Ferm, Deane William,/Third World liber at
BT83.57 .F465 1986 C.1 STACKS 1986

BT
83.57
F465
1986

Ferm, Deane
William, 1927-

Third World
liberation
theologies

DATE DUE

+BT83.57 .F465 1986

THIRD WORLD
LIBERATION THEOLOGIES

An Introductory Survey

Deane William Ferm

COLLEGE FOR HUMAN SERVICES
LIBRARY
345 HUDSON STREET
NEW YORK, NY 10014

ORBIS BOOKS

Maryknoll, New York 10545

Third Printing, March 1988

The Catholic Foreign Mission Society of America (Maryknoll) recruits and trains people for overseas missionary service. Through Orbis Books Maryknoll aims to foster the international dialogue that is essential to mission. The books published, however, reflect the opinions of their authors and are not meant to represent the official position of the society.

© 1986 by Deane William Ferm
Published by Orbis Books, Maryknoll, NY 10545
Manufactured in the United States of America
All rights reserved

Manuscript Editors: Stephen Scharper and William E. Jerman

Library of Congress Cataloging in Publication Data

Ferm, Deane William, 1927-
  Third World liberation theologies.

  Bibliography: p.
  Includes index.
  1. Liberation theology—History. 2. Theology,
Doctrinal—Developing countries—History—20th
century. I. Title.
BT83.57.F465   1985   230′.09172′4   85-15534
ISBN 0-88344-515-8 (pbk.)

To Debra,

Who Continues To Liberate Me

Contents

Chapter 3,
African Liberation Theology   **59**

Chapter 4,
Asian Liberation Theology   **76**

Introduction

Liberation theology, most observers would agree, has been the most significant theological development since the mid-1960s. Appearing in a multitude of forms throughout the Third World, it has provoked both controversy and confusion. Is it really theology? Does it advocate violence? Does it baptize Marxism? What does it say about God?

The purpose of this book is to survey the various manifestations of liberation theology throughout the Third World.* I have focused on leading theologians and have explored how they agree with and differ from one another. Obviously in a book of this size one cannot do justice to every work and every theologian, or even mention all the important figures. But I do believe that anyone who reads this book will have some understanding of what Third World liberation theology is all about. A companion volume, *Third World Liberation Theologies: A Reader,* allows many of these theologians to speak for themselves.

What is meant by the term "liberation theology"? A definition acceptable to everyone would be as difficult to formulate as would a precise characterization of theology itself. It seems to me, however, that liberation theology has two major components. First, it stresses liberation from all forms of human oppression: social, economic, political, racial, sexual, environmental, religious. We shall discover that Third World liberation theology has many different emphases depending on where it has emerged. For example, one could roughly generalize that Latin American liberation theology focuses on social, political, and economic oppression; South African liberation theology highlights racism; Asian liberation theology, in its pluralistic religious setting, strongly urges positive dialogue with the other major living religions.

The second component of liberation theology is its insistence that theology must be truly indigenous. For this reason liberation theology coming out of Peru cannot be merely transported to Sri Lanka or South Korea. We shall see, for example, that most African theologians outside South Africa, in their concern to take the local cultural setting seriously, have shown far greater interest in uncovering their native religious roots than do their Latin American

---

*I shall not here enter into the question, Is the term "Third World" pejorative? I use it in its customary meaning: "Third World" refers to Latin America, Africa, and most parts of Asia; "First World" refers to North America and the NATO countries of western Europe; "Second World" refers to the Soviet Union and the Warsaw Pact countries of eastern Europe.

1

counterparts, who have, for the most part, remained within their Christian (usually Roman Catholic) moorings. As one might expect, this issue of indigenization provokes increasing debate among Third World theologians.

In this survey, Latin American liberation theology receives considerably more attention than do its African and Asian counterparts. The reason for this is threefold. First, Latin American liberation theology, which gathered considerable momentum after Vatican II, virtually exploded between the meetings of Latin American bishops at Medellín, Columbia, in 1968, and Puebla, Mexico, in 1979. African and Asian liberation theologies, on the other hand, did not gain prominence until the mid-1970s. Secondly, literature produced by Latin American theologians, as a result of its early recognition, became more readily available in translation to North Americans than that emanating from Asia and Africa. Fortunately, this imbalance has begun to correct itself. It is important, however, that we not consider African and Asian liberation theologies to be mere offshoots of Latin American liberation theologies, any more than the Latin Americans are but stepchildren of European political theologies and theologies of hope, as some critics charge. Thirdly, this book is by intent an introduction for English-speaking readers. For this reason I have concentrated on translated rather than untranslated and, in many cases, virtually inaccessible material. In this regard I express my deep appreciation to Orbis Books for the work it has done to make Third World liberation theology available to a much larger audience.

If I can accomplish two goals in this book, I shall be satisfied. First, I want to show that Third World liberation theology is not monolithic; it contains as much variety as does any other contemporary theology. Secondly, I hope that this survey will encourage readers to dig more deeply into this fascinating theological area, so rapidly expanding and diversifying. For this reason I have made reference to important supplementary material in the endnotes and have included a select bibliography.

This book would never have been written without the advice of many individuals too numerous to mention here. But I must single out the Orbis team—Stephen Scharper, John Eagleson, William Jerman and especially Philip Scharper—for sticking with me through thick and thin. No one, however, deserves more praise than my wife, Debra. I never would have completed this task without her wisdom, her encouragement, and her tender loving care.

CHAPTER ONE

The Background of Liberation Theology

LATIN AMERICA: A BRIEF HISTORICAL OVERVIEW

How does one begin the history of a territory so vast and complex, and about which so little is known, whose many faces have changed and continue to change through the years in such convulsive ways? Only toward the end of the nineteenth century did major historical studies of Latin America emerge, yet even they appear sketchy and imprecise by the standards of modern historical research. Indeed, can one write about "Latin American history" or the "Latin American experience" with any more justification than one can claim to extrapolate the "North American view" or the "European approach"? Latin American history comprises a tangled skein of traditions, customs, and cultures continually changing as they intersect with one another.

For more than four centuries, the Catholic Church has been playing a dominant role in that history, proclaiming a gospel of salvation transmitted through Spanish and Portuguese earthen vessels. The violent history of Latin American colonialization, in which the Catholic Church figured prominently, is of central importance for anyone attempting to grasp Latin American theological reflections on liberation.

Europe began its conquest of what is now called Latin America with Christopher Columbus's "discovery" of the West Indies in 1492. Two years later, Pope Alexander VI negotiated the Treaty of Tordesillas, which divided the New World between Spain and Portugal, and set the stage for "patronage"—royal control over the church in the mission lands the two European nations would colonize. Church and state worked hand in hand in the settlement of Latin America. Spain and Portugal imposed their own feudal structures on the newly conquered territory. The native Amerindians became Christians, usually under duress, but they never really rejected their own indigenous cultures and religions.

The sixteenth century saw the rapid expansion of Christian missions as Spain and Portugal conquered more and more Latin American soil. When the Aztecs of Mexico, the Incas of Peru, and their counterparts in other areas were subdued, Dominicans and Franciscans followed closely behind. Most of these early missionaries viewed the indigenes as ignorant children desperately in need of Christian instruction. They preferred to make converts by peaceful means, but would resort to force if necessary. The clerical conquerors were as ambitious as the military, one as violent as the other in their methods of conversion or control. As Penny Lernoux notes:

> From the moment Columbus set foot in the New World cross and sword had been indistinguishable. Priests and conquistadors divided the plunder in people and land—it was a toss-up which was the greedier. And long before Latin America's military regimes installed their torture chambers the Inquisition was at work with whip and rock. By the time of the wars of independence at the beginning of the nineteenth century, the Church was the largest landowner in Latin America. It was also the most conservative political force on the continent.[1]

To be sure, other scholars dispute this view. Renato Poblete claims that "in Latin America the actual transition from paganism to Christianity was accomplished with a minimum of struggle." He even claims:

> In all respects this was a golden age for the Latin American church, and its splendor, now dimmed, can still be glimpsed in the magnificent cathedrals of Mexico, Quito, and Lima.[2]

These cathedrals are indeed splendid, but at what human price?

Some missionaries, however, stand out as exemplary in their treatment of the Amerindians and in their valiant attempts to convince state and church authorities to change their cruel ways.

Notable among these priests was Bartolomé de Las Casas, who arrived in Santo Domingo in 1514. Although a slave holder himself, Las Casas later freed his African slaves and sought to evangelize the Amerindians in a peaceful way. Until his death in 1566 he pled the cause of the natives, both in the New World and in Spain, before civil and church authorities, earning him the title "defender of the Indians." For many today he is the Moses of Latin American liberation theology.

There were, however, other prominent clerics who championed the cause of the native peoples. Antonio de Valdivieso, for example, bishop of Nicaragua during the 1540s, tried to persuade Spanish authorities to end the brutal treatment of the Amerindians. He was killed for his efforts. Juan del Valle relinquished his comfortable position as professor of arts at the University of Salamanca, Spain, to become bishop of Popayan in Colombia in the 1550s and spent the remainder of his life trying to stop maltreatment of the natives. These are but three examples of courageous missionaries who, in the words of Enrique Dussel:

risked everything, committing themselves without reservation, suffering expulsion from their dioceses, imprisonment, deportations, and even death in behalf of the Indians who were being violently oppressed and exploited by the Spanish colonizers. Las Casas advocated "evangelism without arms," which signifies today liberation not as a struggle against subversion but in favor of the humanization of those unjustly treated: the Indians, the mestizo, the peasant, the laborer, the simple people, the poor, and the uneducated.[3]

The Spanish and Portuguese conquest of Latin America did not usher in a golden age in the treatment of the indigenous inhabitants, but it was not without its martyrs and prophets, whom the liberation theologians of today regard as their progenitors.

The latter half of the sixteenth century saw the church consolidating its strength as bishops and priests began to meet in provincial councils to coordinate their evangelization programs. Fifteen such councils were held over the next two hundred years as church leaders developed catechetical instruction and rules of behavior for the converts—rules more often in keeping with Spanish customs than native practices. By the beginning of the seventeenth century, 120,000 Spaniards faced 12 million Amerindians scattered over 12 million square miles. In some areas Spanish cruelty continued unabated. Noel Leo Erskine reports that native Jamaicans at the time of the arrival of Christopher Columbus totaled roughly 60 thousand. A century later the population had diminished to 1,500, only 74 of whom were pureblood natives.[4]

Latin American society was divided into several classes. At the top were the leaders of both state and church, most of them coming directly from Spain. Their offspring, born in the New World, constituted the second level, and generally filled government positions. Below them, in turn, were the Spanish urban masses, then the Amerindians, most of whom lived in rural areas, and, at the very bottom of the social ladder, mestizos and blacks.

The history of the church from 1500 to the late 1700s in this class-divided Latin America was linked to the rise and fall of the Spanish government, its loss of colonial control, and the weakening of its power over the affairs of the Latin American church. By the early part of the nineteenth century, a growing bone of contention was the tremendous wealth amassed by the church. In Peru, for example, at the time of independence, "there was scarcely an estate of any size which did not belong in whole or in part to the clerics."[5] As the struggle for independence from Spain and Portugal increased, a major issue became that of control over the wealth of the church. As the former colonial governments achieved their independence in the eighteenth century, they sought the same control over the church that Spain had previously enjoyed, a strategy that strained relations between the Vatican and these countries for decades.

By the end of the nineteenth century the expanding British empire, extending its economic and political influence in Latin America, acted with a heavy hand in exploiting these struggling nations, only to be outdone in the twentieth century by the emerging power of the United States. Thus, although in spirit most of the Latin American countries gained political independence by the beginning of the twentieth century, in point of fact economic dependence on Great Britain and later the United States became so overwhelming that the countries of the southern hemisphere became subservient to their economic overlords.

The twentieth century has seen the phenomenal growth of the population of Latin America. From 63 million in 1900, the figure had risen to 100 million by 1924 and 200 million by 1960. By the year 2000 the population is expected to exceed 600 million. In a single century the population of Latin America will have increased tenfold. The social problems precipitated by this population explosion are absolutely staggering. Further, one-third of the Catholics in the world today live in Latin America—expected to increase to one-half by the year 2000.

An added problem for the Catholic Church is that Latin America has the lowest proportion of priests per population in the world. Although an estimated 95 percent of the population of Latin America has been baptized into the Catholic Church, in certain areas—rural Peru and Venezuela, for example— the severe shortage of priests means that residents of those areas do not have Mass even once a week. This has led one church observer to exclaim:

> Sometimes I am led to think that Jesus Christ did not initiate the sacraments of the Eucharist and of penance for the people of Latin America, for they simply do not have the opportunities to receive them.[6]

In recent decades an increasing and significant minority of members of the Catholic Church have shown growing concern for the staggering problems of the social order. Catholic Action had its beginnings in Argentina in 1930, in Peru in 1935, and in Bolivia in 1938, spreading quickly to other countries. Lay persons, prompted by the lack of priests, assumed positions of leadership and sought to apply Catholic teachings to social problems.

THE PREDAWN OF LIBERATION THEOLOGY

From 1930 to 1960, the Catholic Church experienced a theological and liturgical revival concentrated especially in the religious orders and seminaries. This ferment surfaced in the general conference of the Latin American episcopacy (CELAM I), which convened in Rio de Janeiro in 1955 with Pope Pius XII in attendance. This conference addressed many issues, not the least of which was the modern role of the church in missions and in the social order. Liberation theology was presaged in Cardinal Adeodato Piazza's reference to Jesus' first sermon to define the proper mission of the church: "The spirit of the Lord has been given to me, for he has anointed me. He has sent me to bring the good news to the poor."

Vatican II

Two major events of the 1960s shook the Catholic Church in Latin America to its foundations: Vatican II and the Medellín conference (CELAM II) of 1968. It is important that we consider both events in some detail and note their impact on Latin America, for these two events, more than any others, gave *official* impetus to the emergence of liberation theology.

Both proponents and critics of liberation theology stress the importance of Vatican II and its convener, Pope John XXIII. Gustavo Gutiérrez of Peru, the leading exponent of Latin American liberation theology, has said that the Medellín conference would not have been possible without Vatican II and Pope John XXIII.[7] In addition, C. Peter Wagner, no friend of liberation theology, has stated:

> When historians evaluate this period a century from now, it may well turn out that Pope John XXIII will have been judged to have had more influence on the Latin American continent than any other man in the twentieth century. Roman Catholicism will never be the same as a result of the council he called and the attitude he infused.[8]

Pope John XXIII convened the council in 1962. It met for two months at a time for the next four years. After the death of John XXIII in 1963, Pope Paul VI continued where his predecessor had left off. Vatican II represents the positive response of the Catholic Church to the challenges of the modern world. Possibly the spirit of openness to all "separated brethren" epitomized by Pope John himself had a greater impact than even the documents themselves.

Nevertheless, one should not underestimate the significance of the Vatican II documents. Of major importance is *Gaudium et Spes* (1965), which emphasizes the special responsibility Christians have toward "those who are poor or in any way afflicted."[9] This document underlines the increasing gap between the haves and have-nots, as well as the universal mandate "to count social necessities among the primary duties of modern man."[10] It denies that the church is bound to any single social, economic, or political system and maintains that what is most important is the wider distribution of economic power. *Gaudium et Spes* recognizes the importance of organized labor and even of the right to strike for just demands, as part of the effort to press for a fairer distribution of goods. It affirms that the church itself, although independent of the political sector, has the right—even the duty—to pass moral judgments on political matters.

Encyclical Support

One finds the same spirit of willingness to confront the new demands of a changing world in the papal encyclicals issued during the 1960s. Pope John

XXIII's *Mater et Magistra* (1961), which builds upon the two landmark social encyclicals *Rerum Novarum* (1891) and *Quadragesimo Anno* (1931), illustrates this point well. In *Quadragesimo Anno*, Pius XI had advanced two basic principles: "practical morality" must govern economic affairs, and the interests of an individual or a society must be subordinate to the common good. He explicitly rejected unregulated competition and the subjugation of any society to the interests of its wealthiest members.

Pope John XXIII went a step further. He agreed with Pius XI that it was wrong for the powerful members of a society to determine the wage scale and he declared unjust any society in which "the human dignity of workers is compromised, or their sense of responsibility is weakened, or their freedom of action is removed."[11] He also shared with Pius XI the conviction that wage earners should share in some way in ownership, management, or profits.[12] And John XXIII dealt with another question that had emerged between the two pontificates: the exploitation of Third World countries. *Mater et Magistra* proclaims the duty of wealthy industrialized nations to help less privileged countries, not only out of a sense of Christian charity or a desire to help the poor, but also because of a *shared responsibility* for the plight of their unfortunate neighbors.

Pope Paul VI built upon the foundation laid by his predecessors, as his encyclical *Populorum Progressio* (1967) indicates. He notes how trips to Latin America and Africa in the early 1960s gave him a firsthand look at the plight of the poor and points out why he had established a pontifical commission "to further the progress of poorer peoples, to encourage social justice among nations, to offer to less developed nations the means whereby they can further their own progress."[13]

In this encyclical the pope writes of "the scandal of glaring inequalities" in both possessions and power, and points out how the Vatican Council insisted on the imperative of expropriating landed estates that were poorly utilized and brought harm to the people.[14] He denounces those who make profit the key motive for economic progress and deplores the fact that "a type of capitalism has been the source of excessive suffering, injustices, and fratricidal conflicts."[15] The pope recognizes the urgency of the situation: "We must make haste; too many are suffering, and the distance is growing that separates the progress of some and the stagnation, not to say the regression, of others."[16] He goes on to say:

> There are certainly situations where injustice cries to heaven. When whole populations destitute of necessities live in a state of dependence barring them from all initiative and responsibility, and all opportunity to advance culturally and share in social and political life, recourse to violence, as a means to right these wrongs to human dignity, is a grave temptation.[17]

Paul VI insists that "the superfluous wealth of rich countries should be placed at the service of poor nations"; otherwise their continued greed will bring down the wrath of the poor.[18] In short, the world, exclaims the pontiff, is sick—sick of luxury and waste in the midst of poverty, and sick of horrendous economic and social inequalities. It is imperative for lay persons to take the initiative in making necessary changes in the customs, laws, and structures of their communities. He ends by declaring:

> All of you who have heard the appeal of suffering people, all of you who are working to answer their cries, you are the apostles of a development which is good and genuine, which is not wealth that is self-centered and sought for its own sake, but rather an economy which is put at the service of man; the bread which is daily distributed to all, as a source of brotherhood and a sign of Providence. . . . Yes, we ask you, all of you, to heed our cry of anguish, in the name of the Lord.[19]

From the publication of *Rerum Novarum* in 1891 to the late 1960s, Catholic social teaching in the form of papal encyclicals and conciliar documents had undergone a steady transformation. There was increasing concern shown for the poor, suffering, and oppressed; for the rights of workers; for the responsibilities that the wealthy nations have for the impoverished; for the defects of capitalism based exclusively on the profit motive; for the role of both church and state in liberating the oppressed. And what area of the world needed to hear this social message more than Latin America, where political power makes the small number of rich even richer and the vast number of poor even poorer?

A major cause of poverty and oppression in Latin America has been and remains the economic policies of the United States government and of multinational corporations—policies that buttress repressive governments. As one observer puts it:

> The basic difference between American imperialism today and American imperialism a century ago is that it is more violent, more far-reaching, and more carefully planned today.[20]

Consider this example. Between 1950 and 1955 the United States invested $2 billion in Latin America, chiefly in new materials and agriculture. From this investment the United States made a profit of $3.5 billion, nearly half of which returned to the United States. As is obvious, a nation that dominates the economy of another nation dominates its political sector as well. For this reason the U.S. government plan for so-called development in Latin America is a sure way to maintain the economic, social, and political status quo. Furthermore, in light of the insistence of protecting national security by military might, it becomes obvious why the U.S. government and multinational corporations will inevitably support political structures that favor their own self-interests above all else. Enrique Dussel spells out the results of such a policy:

It is not surprising . . . that since 1960 the amount of violence has dramatically increased on the one hand by the military governments supported by the Pentagon and the national police (with their methods of torture often taught by the United States experts in counterinsurgency) and on the other hand by the rural and urban guerillas. With the death of John Kennedy and the failure of the heralded Alliance for Progress program, the United States began to support all the forces in Latin America that called themselves "anti-Communists," a euphemism for counterrevolution, that is, those governments that directed their efforts against the popular revolutions through neo-colonial militarism.[21]

With this portrait in mind one can understand why more and more Latin Americans mistrust "foreign aid" programs and "alliances for progress," and wonder whether the only way to break the spiral of violence supported by entrenched political and economic structures is literally to break the structures themselves. After all, as John F. Kennedy used to warn us, those who make peaceful revolution impossible make violent revolution inevitable.

For a long time Latin America had been ripe for massive social revolution. When the social teachings of Vatican II and the social encyclicals of Pope John XXIII and Paul VI began to trickle down into Latin America, a small but growing number of bishops, priests, and lay persons found confirmation of what they themselves had come to see as the role of the church in building a new social order. After all, six hundred bishops from Latin America had attended the opening proceedings of Vatican II in 1962, and they and their advisers could not help but be deeply committed to the social documents that they and their colleagues had supported. Meanwhile, at the annual regional meetings of the Latin American episcopacy, the implications of Vatican II and the papal encyclicals—in particular, the more recent *Populorum Progressio*—were thoroughly discussed.

In 1967 bishops from Latin America, Africa, and Asia issued "A Letter to the Peoples of the Third World," which maintained that revolution can be an appropriate means to overcome injustice, and stated that the rich were inciters of violence. More and more bishops, priests, and lay persons had come to realize that in order to remedy the desperate poverty and injustices of the masses, Latin American nations had to eliminate political and economic domination and create their own destiny in the community of nations. Thus, beginning in the 1960s, a new era began for the church in Latin America, an era marked by a growing concern for the poor, resistance to the privileged few, distrust of the established order, and protest against the prevailing structures of the social order. It was in this atmosphere that liberation theology was born.

Medellín

The second major event in the 1960s for the Catholic Church in Latin America was the General Conference of the Latin American episcopacy

(CELAM II) held in 1968 in Medellín, Colombia. Enrique Dussel considers CELAM II the "Vatican II of Latin America,"[22] and Gustavo Gutiérrez points to the year 1968 as the birthdate of Latin American liberation theology.[23] What the Medellín conference did above all else was to focus attention on the Latin American situation, particularly the pervasive human injustice and oppression. What does God have to say and what ought the church as God's agent do about all this suffering?

The theme of the conference was "The Church in the Present-Day Transformation of Latin America in the Light of the Council."[24] Sixteen documents were produced, ranging in subject matter from justice, peace, education, and youth to liturgy, lay movements, the mass media, and the poverty of the church. In reading the documents, it becomes apparent that the majority of the 145 cardinals, bishops, and priests who attended this conference had been deeply and positively influenced by Vatican II—many of them had been present at it—as well as by Pope Paul VI's encyclical *Populorum Progressio* of 1967, which had directly addressed the Latin American situation. At Medellín these church leaders were determined to spell out forcefully the role of the church in confronting the social and political problems that they knew first-hand.

The heart of the Medellín documents can be summarized in two of its passages:

> By its own vocation Latin America will undertake its liberation at the cost of whatever sacrifice.[25]
>
> The Lord's distinct commandment to "evangelize the poor" ought to bring us to a distribution of resources and apostolic personnel that effectively gives preference to the poorest and most needy sectors.[26]

Medellín is the cradle of liberation theology. It is a clear and unambiguous assertion that the church should exercise a "preferential option for the poor"—an ideal that has become the hallmark of liberation theology. However, the documents do not represent a unanimous point of view. Both proponents and opponents of liberation theology can find passages to bolster their own positions. And the documents are far more impressive in analyzing conditions than in proposing solutions. But what Medellín did accomplish, in the words of Phillip Berryman, was "to give a green light to creative minorities all over the continent whose participation in the liberation struggle has led to a radicalization of the themes presented in Medellín."[27]

Basic Christian Communities

Although Vatican II and Medellín were important catalysts, they did not produce liberation theology. Liberation theology emerged from the lives of the poor and oppressed in Latin America and, in particular, from the small basic Christian communities (CEBs—*comunidades eclesiales de base*) of the dispossessed—creative minorities seeking to relate their Christian convictions to their everyday lives. These small communities, mostly in rural areas and on the outer edges of the cities, are formed by simple Christians who gather together to worship God and live out their responsibility to make Christ real in their lives. In the words of Alvaro Barreiro:

> The CEBs are trying to live in a demanding way and under the extremely difficult conditions of their environment, the good news which they have accepted; celebrating it jubilantly in worship and proclaiming it courageously to those who have not yet heard it. . . . When the oppressed poor accept the gospel as good news of liberation, and actually strive to become liberated from the oppression that is being suffered, they are, ipso facto, battling against the sin of the oppressor, inviting the latter to conversion. . . . The great revelation of the gospel of Jesus Christ and the radical innovation of the good news that he brings lies in his preferential love for the poor and sinners.[28]

CEBs have mushroomed all over Latin America. By the end of the 1970s approximately eighty thousand such communities existed in Brazil alone. The CEBs are the very stuff out of which liberation theology grows, for they are the "poor in action" of which liberation theology is but a reflection. Many of these communities use educational methods developed by Paulo Freire. He introduced "conscientization," a process by which persons are made aware of how important it is to integrate their religious faith with their day-to-day political and social lives. In his widely influential book, *Pedagogy of the Oppressed*, Freire writes:

> The central problem is this: How can the oppressed, as divided, unauthentic beings, participate in developing the pedagogy of their liberation? . . . The starting point for organizing the program content of education or political action must be the present, existential, concrete situation, reflecting the aspirations of the people.[29]

Three Outstanding Figures

Out of the basic community movement have emerged numerous courageous individuals who, in their battle against injustice and oppression, have incarnated the basic features of liberation theology. Three such individuals will be singled out here as representative, but many more could be included.

Ernesto "Che" Guevara

"Che" Guevara, a medical student from Argentina, became radicalized through his participation in the Cuban revolution and joined the opposition forces in Bolivia in their attempt to overthrow the reactionary government. In

1967 he was captured, tortured, and executed by members of the Bolivian army. In the early 1960s he stated:

> The present moment may or may not be the proper one for starting the struggle, but we cannot harbor any illusions, we have no right to do so, that our freedom can be obtained without fighting. . . . Our every action is a battle cry against imperialism and a call for the peoples' unity against the great enemy of mankind: the United States of America. Whenever death may surprise us, it will be welcome, provided that this, our battle cry, reaches some receptive ears, that another hand be extended to take up our weapons and that other men come forward to intone our funeral dirge with the staccato of machine guns and new cries of battle and victory.[30]

Camilo Torres

Camilo Torres was a priest from a prosperous family in Colombia who changed his social and political views markedly while studying sociology at Louvain, where he was a classmate of Gustavo Gutiérrez. Torres later left a university post and joined Colombian revolutionary forces. Prior to his participation in the struggle, he stopped performing his priestly duties, declaring:

> I have ceased to say Mass [in order] to practice love for people in temporal, economic and social spheres. When the people have nothing against me, when they have carried out the revolution, then I will return to offering Mass, God willing. . . . I think that in this way I follow Christ's injunction . . . "Leave thy gifts upon the altar and go first to be reconciled to thy brothers."[31]

Torres was killed in 1966. His death made him a hero of the new young left and the names of Torres and Guevara became household words throughout Latin America.

Dom Hélder Câmara

Dom Hélder Câmara was ordained a priest in 1931, served as auxiliary bishop of Rio de Janeiro from 1952 to 1964, and later became archbishop of Recife in northeastern Brazil, a position he held until his retirement in 1985. His intense social activism, combined with an equally strong devotional life, merited for him the unofficial title "bishop of the poor." Dom Hélder was instrumental in founding the National Conference of the Bishops of Brazil (CNBB), and was a major figure in the development of liberation theology. Completely unassuming ("I am becoming one of the voiceless poor of Brazil," he once said), he has devoted his life to trying to arrest the "spiral of violence" that has consumed so much of Latin America. He was one of the first to appreciate the creative possibilities to be found in a socialist system of government, noting as early as 1956:

> The union of socialism and democracy means . . . that authentic human construction of socialism is not possible without the simultaneous implantation of a real socialist democracy.[32]

In 1966 he was the instigator in drafting a statement signed by fifteen Latin American bishops committing the church to the poor. No narrow ideologue, Dom Hélder Câmara has been an eloquent spokesman for the poor and oppressed. His entire credo can be summarized in one simple sentence: "The protests of the poor are the voice of God."[33]

Christians for Socialism

Another major development that fed the emergence of liberation theology was the Christians for Socialism movement, which had its beginnings in Chile in 1971.[34] At a meeting of eighty priests from throughout Latin America, the movement drafted a document that stated:

> As Christians we do not see any incompatibility between Christianity and socialism. Quite the contrary is true . . . it is necessary to destroy the prejudice and mistrust that exists between Christians and Marxists.[35]

This statement goes beyond the Medellín conference, which tried to steer a middle course between capitalism and socialism. The same theme surfaced at a convention of four hundred Latin American Christians held in Santiago, Chile in 1972, where the final document affirmed:

> The economic and social structures of our Latin American countries are grounded on oppression and injustice, which in turn is a result of our capitalist dependence on the great power centers. . . . We commit ourselves to the task of fashioning socialism because it is our objective conclusion . . . that this is the only effective way to combat imperialism and to break away from our situation of dependence. . . . There is a growing awareness that revolutionary Christians must form a strategic allegiance with Marxists within the liberation process on this continent. . . . Socialism presents itself as the only acceptable option for getting beyond a class-based society.[36]

This "preference for the poor by way of socialism" met fierce resistance from the established political and religious structures. Governments considered this socialist credo a distinct threat to the capitalist forces that kept them in power. And the official teachings of the church had yet to acknowledge any merit in *any* form of socialism. That would occur less than a decade later in

Pope John Paul II's 1981 encyclical *Laborem Exercens*.

The Christians for Socialism movement in Latin America did not survive as an independent force, but the seeds sown by it continued to germinate. Its importance lies in its harsh criticism of the evils and abuses of a capitalist system that favors a wealthy minority and provides but a few crumbs for the oppressed majority.

For liberation theologians, the voices of the poor are indeed, in Dom Hélder's words, "the voice of God." These theologians are convinced that social reform *will* come to Latin America in one way or another. Their primary mission is to promote this inevitable social reform in a Christian context. It is to these theologians that I now turn.

CHAPTER TWO

Latin American Liberation Theology

Writing in 1971, Enrique Dussel stated that Latin America had not yet produced any leading theologian.[1] This situation has changed rapidly! In the 1970s and 1980s, Latin American theologians have written an abundance of books and articles that have led to the conclusion that their authors are at the forefront of the making of contemporary theology. All that I can attempt here is to point out the main themes of some of these theologians, knowing that a survey of this kind cannot do full justice to their creative insights and that regretably some important theologians will not be included.

EXPLORING THE MAJOR THEMES

Gustavo Gutiérrez

Most observers consider Gustavo Gutiérrez of Peru the preeminent Latin American liberation theologian. His *Teología de la liberación,* published in 1971 (English translation, *A Theology of Liberation,* published in 1973), has been hailed as the Magna Carta of liberation theology.[2]

Gutiérrez was born in 1928 in Lima, Peru. He studied for a time at the San Marcos University Medical School in Lima, where he took a particular interest in psychiatry. Later he felt called to the priesthood. His pursuit of theological studies took him to Louvain, Lyons, and Rome. He returned to Peru to accept a teaching position at the Catholic University in Lima. Ordained a priest in 1959, he moved to Rimac, a slum area of Lima, where he continues to reside. He teaches in the Department of Theology and Social Sciences at the Catholic Pontifical University in Lima and serves as director of the Bartolomé de Las Casas Center in the heart of Rimac.

Of Amerindian ancestry, Gutiérrez had experienced the pangs of discrimination in his early years—an experience that prompted him to become a political activist in his undergraduate years. His encounter with daily suffering in Rimac strengthened his resolve to focus his priestly concerns on the plight of the oppressed. This commitment was also reinforced by his discovery of the writings of the early Spanish liberator Bartolomé de Las Casas.

During the 1960s, Gutiérrez became increasingly disenchanted with his formal theological training. In Europe, theology had been presented primarily as an intellectual discipline, more attuned to the life of the mind than to the actual living conditions of the poor. As a priest to and of the poor, he came to see that theology—indeed the Christian faith itself—made no sense unless it somehow came to grips with the oppression and violence endured by those whom he was called to serve. During the decade of the 1960s, Gutiérrez encountered other priests who felt as he did—that the theology they had been taught was irrelevant to the poor with whom they lived. One such priest was Camilo Torres, Gutiérrez's fellow student at Louvain, who became radicalized in his ministry to the poor and, as we have already noted, was eventually murdered for his "subversive" activities.

According to Gutiérrez, liberation theology, as a self-conscious movement, was born in 1968, the year that he had gathered with like-minded priests in Lima and later at the episcopal conference in Medellín. Gutiérrez was an active participant at Medellín, serving as the principal author of the document on peace. He also attended the follow-up conferences in Switzerland in 1969 and Colombia in 1970.

It was during this period that Gutiérrez wrote *A Theology of Liberation*. The book was, in essence, a reflection on what he had learned firsthand from his daily encounters with his people during the preceding decade. It is important to go into some detail on the content of this widely influential volume, which has been translated into nine languages and continues to sell over 3,000 copies a year in its English edition.

A Theology of Liberation is Gustavo Gutiérrez's answer to the question, What is the proper role of theology and of the theologian in the attempt to be faithful both to the Christian gospel and to the poor of Latin America? Historically, Gutiérrez notes, theology has served a variety of purposes. One model has emphasized wisdom and understanding. According to this model, the primary task of theology is to comprehend the nature of reality and, further, to provide a reasoned interpretation of the divine revelation entrusted to the church. Thus, theology serves both to strengthen the faith of the believers and to make Christianity intellectually convincing to nonbelievers. Another important theological model has stressed spiritual enlightenment and sought to bring the believer into a close relationship with Christ.

Gutiérrez does not wish to do away with either of these models but rather to transcend them. He suggests a vision of theology drawn from Augustine's *The City of God* and Augustine's attempt to relate the Christian faith to the everyday lives of the Christians of his turbulent times.

In this view, the *primary* task of theology changes from that of convincing the nonbeliever of the "truths" of the Christian faith to that of freeing the oppressed from their inhuman living conditions. From this perspective the "truth" of theology becomes that of the liberation of the oppressed. Thus, theology does not produce Christian faith; rather, theology responds to the conditions in which human beings live. Theology begins with persons—with their historical situation of oppression and poverty. The *second act* of theology becomes "critical reflection on praxis." Theology begins with grass-roots communities, those thousands of small groups of Christians all over Latin America, who come together to confront their injustices and through Bible study seek to overcome their oppression and find a new life in Christ. It is their *concrete, everyday prayerful action and reflection,* their response to their own oppressive situation—in short, their *praxis*—that produces theology. This way of doing theology was not what Gutiérrez had learned in his formal theological studies and in this sense it constitutes an original perspective. The responsibility of theology now becomes that of *changing* the world—not primarily that of *understanding* it—and of joining the struggle against oppression and poverty; in a word, to exercise a "preference for the poor."

In his analysis of the causes of Latin American poverty and oppression, Gutiérrez calls into question the concept of *development* as a solution to the problem—that is, the conviction that foreign countries, such as the United States, can develop the living conditions of the poor and oppressed in Latin America through economic investment. What this development model has invariably meant is that the wealthy countries, in their "development" of the "underdeveloped" countries, get richer and the poor get poorer. The First World reaps the financial benefits of its investment in the Third World. For this reason Gutiérrez rejects the development model and embraces the notion of liberation, a much more radical concept for him, implying complete economic and political independence for the Third World. He insists, as did Medellín, that Latin Americans must take their destiny into their own hands. The liberation of Latin America will not be achieved by foreign interests.

Gutiérrez uses the term "liberation" in three senses. First, liberation means freedom from oppressive economic, social, and political conditions. Secondly, liberation means that human beings take over control of their own historical destiny. Thirdly, liberation includes emancipation from sin and the acceptance of new life in Christ. This is the Christian dimension, which, Gutiérrez insists, is essential to the full meaning of liberation. When Gutiérrez uses the term "liberation," it is important that we interpret it with reference to all three meanings. Too often his critics focus only on the first meaning, and in so doing they fail to do him justice.

Gutiérrez believes that the most important theological task in Latin America is the liberation of the oppressed in all three meanings of the term "liberation." Such full-scale liberation, he contends, can be achieved only if there is an honest acknowledgment of the violence spewn by the present political and social system, as well as a serious and sustained effort on the part of the church to confront and overcome this violence. Too often the church has by design or default aligned itself with the political and social status quo, thereby condoning the violence and injustice. The church today must admit its complicity and change sides. Neutrality is not possible. As Gutiérrez contends:

A large part of the Church is in one way or another linked to those who wield economic and political power in today's world. This applies to its position in the opulent and oppressive countries as well as in the poor countries, as in Latin America, where it is tied to the exploiting classes.[3]

In his later book, *We Drink from Our Own Wells* (a phase he borrows from Bernard of Clairvaux), Gutiérrez stresses the point that liberation is an all-embracing process that "leaves no dimension of human life untouched." An encounter with the Lord" is the necessary point of departure "for a life according to the Spirit."

At the core of this encounter is the life of prayer, which is "an expression of faith and trust in the Lord . . . it takes place in the context of the love that we know to be marked in its very source of gratuitousness." This is not to suggest that Gutiérrez has departed from his basic concern that Christianity must show a preference for the poor (because Jesus did) and that theology must be a reflection of the life of the oppressed. Rather, he affirms—and he has been consistent on this point—that political, social, and economic liberation must emanate from a spirituality of liberation, a life of prayer. Prayer is the feeding ground for theological reflection.

Gutiérrez discerns in the everyday lives of the basic Christian communities of the poor a rich resource in discerning the proper relationship between spiritual and material poverty. Through his encounter with these communities, he has also realized that a life of prayer and total commitment to Christ must be the foundation for the spiritual journey of every Christian. *We Drink from Our Own Wells* should go a long way in setting the record straight on what Gutiérrez has always meant by "liberation theology." It is also significant that in this book the Bible gets top billing (almost 400 references in 171 pages) and Marx gets no mention at all.[4]

In *A Theology of Liberation* and many of his other writings, Gutiérrez insists that the inherent weakness of any capitalist system is its inability to liberate the oppressed, because its profit orientation impels it to discourage Third World countries from taking the initiative to develop their own industrial capabilities. Consequently, the countries of the Third World remain pawns "useful only for high production through the exploitation of the labor force."[5] But Gutiérrez is careful not to insist that socialism is necessarily the answer, for socialism, like capitalism, is subject to many different interpretations. Indeed, Gutiérrez insists that liberation must never be equated with any social system. Yet he does believe that in achieving liberation from foreign capitalist domination, socialism "represents the most fruitful and far-reaching approach."[6] Even this, however, requires further qualification. Gutiérrez does not recommend a socialism imported from the First World, but one indigenous to Latin America.

In the development of a new kind of socialism the church and other concerned parties should utilize the social sciences as a way of understanding the present social order and effecting necessary changes. To this end, Gutiérrez points to the large number of younger priests who have been deeply influenced by the teachings of Vatican II, the papal encyclicals, and the Medellín conference and who, by their identification with the cause of the poor and oppressed, have come to see the importance of their own involvement in the process of social and political change. Indeed, bishops and priests from the most poverty-stricken areas of Latin America have become the most vocal critics of the "institutionalized violence" so endemic throughout Latin America. Once again, Gutiérrez insists, church involvement in politics is nothing new; what is new is that many priests and lay persons are joining the oppressed in their struggle against domination and exploitation.

Although Gutiérrez does not minimize the importance of the recent involvement on the part of the church on the side of the poor, he does insist that full and authentic liberation will never be achieved until the oppressed themselves lead the way. In fact, this latter affirmation is the linchpin of Gutiérrez's theology. Liberation is never a gift from an oppressor, but only a continuing struggle on the part of the oppressed. Liberation theology must always begin from the grass roots. The basic communities of the poor themselves must take the initiative in their struggle for a new social order.

Gutiérrez sees a certain affinity between liberation theology and the European political theology and theology of hope. These European theologies recognize the importance of eradicating systemic evil and discerning God as the liberator involved in the political process. But Gutiérrez faults these theologies for their inability to comprehend the depth of the oppression, poverty, and institutionalized violence found in Latin America. One can no more import European theology to Latin America than one can export Latin American liberation theology to North America. Gutiérrez even shies away from the phrase "theology of revolution" on the grounds that it seems to presuppose a commitment to revolution and even violence.[7]

Gutiérrez also stresses the crucial relationship between salvation and liberation. He would argue that in the deepest sense they are one and the same. Salvation is not something to be achieved in another world. It embraces the fullness of life in this world. Salvation is not "pie in the sky by and by." It is the eradication of injustice, violence, and oppression. For this reason liberation is salvation.

I noted earlier how for Gutiérrez one important meaning of liberation is the overcoming of sin and the acceptance of new life in Christ. It is important to add that Gutiérrez grounds his view of liberation in scripture. The biblical drama is in reality the story of God's initiative in seeking human liberation. There are two pivotal points in this drama: the exodus, God's liberation of the Israelites from slavery, and the coming of Christ, who seeks to liberate all human beings from their oppression. Jesus as liberator confronted the oppressors of his day. In consequence, he was martyred as a subversive who had attacked the political and social status quo. The good news of the resurrection is that liberation is for everyone, because the resurrection is God's promise that justice will triumph, a promise reenacted in the celebration of the Eucharist.

Equally important for Gutiérrez are the exodus and the Christ event as political actions on the part of God. God is not a state manager pulling strings from on high, but rather the great liberator, who became human for our sake and whose constant involvement in the struggle for human justice makes it possible for human beings to fulfill their destiny in a just society. We encounter God in the historical process as we encounter other persons. Gutiérrez takes pains to point out the contention of the Hebrew prophets that to know God is to do justice and that to follow Christ means to serve the needy. In Gutiérrez's words:

> It is not enough to say that love of God is inseparable from the love of one's neighbor. It must be added that love of God is unavoidably expressed *through* love of one's neighbor.[8]

The church, as the agent of Christ, has the heavy obligation to enter the political arena on the side of the needy. But this does not mean, as Gutiérrez's critics sometimes charge, that the church is but one more political instrument. To evangelize through the political process does not thereby reduce the church to the political realm. Rather, the political process is one inescapable dimension of total liberation. Class struggle becomes unavoidable, even for the church, because those in power make that struggle inevitable by keeping the lower classes in submission.

Gutiérrez is particularly sensitive to the charge that he had reduced Christianity to politics. In his later writings he addresses this issue. In his article, "Liberation Praxis and Christian Faith," for example, he poses the question, Are we reducing the Christian faith to the political realm? He answers:

> Yes, in the case of those who use it to serve the interests of those in power; no, in the case of those who denounce that usage as the basis of its message of liberation and gratuitous divine love. Yes, in the case of those who place themselves and the Gospel in the hands of the mighty of the world; no, in the case of those who identify themselves with the poor Christ and seek to establish solidarity with the dispossessed on this continent. Yes, in the case of those who keep it shackled to an ideology that serves the capitalist system; no, in the case of those who have been set free by the gospel message and then seek to liberate it from that same captivity. Yes, in the case of those who wish to neutralize Christ's liberation by restricting or reducing it to a purely spiritual plane that has nothing to do with the concrete world of human beings; no, in the case of those who believe that Christ's salvation is so total and radical that nothing escapes it.[9]

Gutiérrez insists that involvement in the political process is a deeply spiritual experience, for it opens up the believer to a totally new awareness of what it means to be human. This point is often missed by his critics, but it rings clear in his writings. To involve ourselves in the political process is to experience the joy of knowing that God is with us, that we can change our lives. To accept our responsibility as political agents for Christ is to acknowledge that this joy, this love, can be truly celebrated only in a human community in which everyone is a full participant.[10]

Gutiérrez recognizes that in the eyes of many traditional theologians liberation theology is not really theology. To the right wing it is "a strange and bastard mixture of theology and sociology, with a generous sprinkling of politics."[11] To the left wing it is not "a scientific effort to respond to modern questions of faith."[12] Gutiérrez would be the first to admit that liberation theology is not the only theological model, but he insists that it is an authentic model and deserves a fair hearing.

Gutiérrez contends that the first act in liberation theology is praxis, but when it comes to the second act, he can be as erudite and analytical as any theologian of his time.[13] He does not deprecate the importance of classic theology, or of thoughtful reflection in general. "Even the poor have the right to think," he maintains.[14]

Gutiérrez sees himself as an "organic intellectual" (originally linked with the people). As such, his responsibility is to keep the two acts of theology together, above all "to keep our feet solidly planted on the earth that gives theology its life." In tying together the goal of liberation and the task of theology he believes that "the liberation process is the greenhouse, the warm, rich planter, of a theology that will open up altogether new perspectives."[15]

Gustavo Gutiérrez is unquestionably the leading figure in Latin American liberation theology, a distinction he would be the first to reject. He would insist that he is only trying to articulate the desperate, inhuman conditions of the poor, that he is a conduit, not a creator, of theology. Gutiérrez is a person of many dimensions—priest, prophet, teacher, political analyst, spiritual leader. But most of all he is a simple man of God seeking in his own way to listen to and answer the cries of the poor and the powerless. They are the ones who receive his undivided attention. Their dignity and humanity are his greatest concern. His entire theological task can be encapsulated in one question:

How can we say to the poor, the exploited classes, to the marginated races, to the despised cultures, to all the minorities, to the nonpersons— how can we say that God is love and say that all of us are, and ought to be in history, sisters and brothers? How can we say this? This is our great question.[16]

Juan Luis Segundo

Juan Luis Segundo is one of the most prolific writers among the Latin American liberation theologians, having authored more than fifteen books. Born in Montevideo, Uruguay, in 1925, Segundo, a Jesuit, studied philosophy in Argentina, received a licentiate in theology at Louvain, Belgium, in 1956, and earned a doctorate of letters from the University of Paris in 1963. Ordained a priest in 1955, he later founded the Peter Faber Pastoral Center in Montevideo and served as its director until it closed in 1975.

Segundo was already spreading the seeds of liberation theology prior to Vatican II and the emergence of European political theology. His early writings—*Función de la Iglesia en la realidad rioplatense* (1962) and *Concepción cristiana del hombre* (1964)—refute the common charge that Latin American liberation theology is the stepchild of European political theology. In stressing the independence of Latin American liberation theology, Segundo faults Rubem Alves for aligning himself too closely with Jürgen Moltmann and other European political theologians. In his writings Segundo has called attention to what he considers the flaws in European political theology, primarily its failure to give sufficient credit to human beings for their political role in fashioning the future and to appreciate the close causal connection between divine and human intervention.

Like Gutiérrez, Segundo views theology not as an academic discipline for scholars, but as the reflection of the real-life experiences of ordinary believers. This approach can be seen in Segundo's five-volume series entitled *A Theology for Artisans of a New Humanity,* a course in theology produced by and for the grassroots communities of the Peter Faber Center during the late 1960s and early 1970s. In this interaction with lay Christians, Segundo focuses on several issues directly related to their daily lives. First is the crisis of the church in the modern world. Vatican II had issued the challenge to the church to enter into dialogue with the world, a challenge that often left the church with the insecure feeling that it had no easy answers to the immense social problems the world faced. Yet, rather than seeing this as a threat, Segundo welcomes this insecurity, insisting that it can liberate the church from a false complacency and enable it to become a "sign of salvation" to encourage Christians to lead more constructive and authentic lives.[17] The church should admit that it does not possess all the answers and then get on with its first order of business, which is serving the people.

Along this same line, Segundo disavows the traditional notion of grace as prepackaged in a sacramental system. He argues that a careful reading of the New Testament reveals that Jesus never intended to institute a formal sacramental system, and he bemoans the fact that this system has played such an important role in the history of the church. Sacraments are indeed important, but primarily as "community gestures and signs," encouraging Christians to get on with the process of liberation. In Segundo's words:

A community gathered together around a liberative paschal message needs signs which fashion it and question it, which imbue it with a sense of responsibility and enable it to create its own word about man's history. This is precisely what the sacraments are—and nothing else but that. Through them God grants and signifies to the Church the grace which is to constitute it truly as such within the most human community.[18]

Another question that Segundo confronts is that of why traditional discussions of the existence and attributes of God seem so nonsensical to the modern believer. Segundo doubts that the early Christian communities showed any particular excitement about the trinitarian controversies that so dominated the attention of ecclesiastical officialdom. Even today interest in that kind of theology is limited to "specialists and 'snobs.' "[19] In the same vein Segundo faults the "death of god" theologians of the 1960s for worrying about God's existence rather than trying to figure out the oppressive human conditions that made God's love so unreal for so many.

Using the Medellín documents as his basis, Segundo argues that, although they may not contain an explicit affirmation of God as Liberator, they do provide the premises for such a conclusion. Segundo's discussion of the "God question" is particularly important for critics of liberation theology who maintain, without warrant, that God is not part of the content of liberation theology. What these critics do not seem to understand is that the whole notion of God has changed. Segundo contrasts the traditional view of God with that of liberation theology:

> When we contemplate a force, a profundity, a being that transcends everything else, it is quite possible that we are not contemplating the Christian God at all. On the other hand, when we or other people dedicate our efforts and our lives to the work of fostering mutual respect and love and unity among men, the end product of all the justice, love and solidarity created by our world relates us infallibly to the Christian God whether we are aware of it or not.[20]

Segundo draws attention to the fact that Christians and atheists have much more in common than most Christians realize, because more often than not the atheist is rejecting an outmoded view of God that Christians too should reject. Segundo argues that atheism is a necessary ingredient of authentic faith, for it keeps us from the human arrogance that makes us think we have God "all wrapped up." For Segundo—as for Alfred North Whitehead—the keynote of idolatry is contentment with the established gods. In Segundo's words, "Our notion of God must never cease to retravel the road which runs from atheism to faith."[21] Here Segundo articulates what has become a major affirmation of Latin American liberation theology: that idolatry—the worship of false gods—is a far greater threat than is atheism. Too often Christians are put in the position of trying to defend a god who not only does not exist, but should not exist.

Segundo's *A Theology for Artisans of a New Humanity* was written during the same period Gutiérrez wrote his *A Theology of Liberation*. Gutiérrez's main purpose was to begin to develop the contours of a full-blown liberation theology in the context of Latin America, but Segundo's work addresses itself more to specific religious concepts—church, grace, sacraments, and concept of God—and how these concepts need to be redefined as authentic reflections of grass-roots communities.

In his subsequent writings, Segundo continues the development of many of these same themes. For example, in his *The Hidden Motives of Pastoral Action,* he insists that if we continue to perpetuate the old notion of the church as engaged in a "numbers game," whereby the strength of the faith is gauged by the number of converts, the church will continue to be irrelevant to the needs of grass-roots communities. But if we are willing to see the church as an agent for the liberation of all peoples, then we will concentrate on changing lives and being open to truths previously hidden from us. Segundo envisages the church of the future as a heroic minority rather than a protective majority that impedes salvation—namely, liberation. Because Segundo suggests that the church should end up being a creative minority, his critics charge him with elitism and even indifference to the needs of the masses. This charge seems unwarranted, however, for all that Segundo is suggesting is that the church act as the leaven that will transform the entire loaf. The interests of the church are the interests of society at large.

In his *The Liberation of Theology,* Segundo develops the theme that liberation theology is based on a new methodology, the "hermeneutic circle":

> The continuing change in our interpretation of the Bible, which is dictated by the continuing change in our present-day reality, both individual and societal. . . . The circular nature of this interpretation stems from the fact that each new reality obliges us to interpret the word of God afresh, to change reality accordingly, and then to go back and reinterpret the word of God again, and so on.[22]

This hermeneutical circle is an ever ongoing process in which we must be willing to lay bare for unending scrutiny our traditional interpretations of scripture as we let scripture and society continually intersect and challenge each other. Segundo also makes use of the terms "hermeneutics of suspicion" or "ideological suspicion"—phrases now used by many liberation theologians— to refer to those dangerous, latent interpretations or ideologies that color our basic assumptions more than we care to admit. According to Segundo, traditional Western theology serves as a perfect example of a theology adapted to the particular ideological interests of dominant social classes. In fact, this theology is so well adapted in that direction that it bears no trace of the interests of oppressed majorities. Segundo strongly rebuts the claims that classic Western theology is devoid of ideology and that it can flourish as "an academic discipline in the security of some chamber immune to the risks of the liberation struggle."[23] For Segundo, theology must shed its false aura of self-proclaimed neutrality and unashamedly become a revolutionary activity bent on the transformation of the social order—a praxis that finds theological method more important even than theological content.

In his development of what might be called a "process methodology," Segundo reveals a close affinity with the views of Pierre Teilhard de Chardin. He quotes with approval Teilhard's contention:

In the world, nothing could ever burst forth as final across the different thresholds successively traversed by evolution (however critical they may be) which has not already existed in an obscure and primordial way.[24]

Segundo shows how the medium is more important than the message in the development of his christology. Unlike many other liberation theologians, Segundo does not politicize Jesus as a radical revolutionary. In fact, he is reluctant to turn Jesus' own political convictions into an ideology normative for all Christians. Segundo readily admits that there can be no faith without ideology—a point that, as we shall see, he takes pains to elaborate in subsequent writings—and thus the question becomes, What ideology works best for Latin America today? What would Christ say and do if he were confronting our own particular situation? Segundo is critical of Míguez Bonino, Leonardo Boff, and others who, in his opinion, make too facile a connection between Jesus' own historical situation and the situation in Latin America today. Drawing on insights from Teilhard, Segundo suggests the inherently changeable nature of christology, focusing more on the "pedagogical intent" of scripture than on its contents.

Another important issue that Segundo addresses in *The Liberation of Theology* is that of the social order best for present-day Latin America. Just as he is wary of too close a connection between Jesus' own political convictions and the situation today, so too is he critical of Hugo Assmann and others who, Segundo believes, suggest that Marxist ideology is essential for the application of Christian faith to social problems in Latin America. Once again, Segundo admits that Christians, wherever they live, cannot avoid political ideologies, but this does not mean that they should ally themselves unequivocally with Marxist ideology any more than they should accept the ideology of the political status quo.

In his discussion of the capitalism-socialism debate, Segundo insists that the discussion not be narrowed to focus on whether Latin America should imitate the society that now exists in either the United States or the Soviet Union. The more appropriate question is, Which system can best be adapted to the unique situation in Latin America? Although Segundo does not wave the banner for either social system *as such*, he does say in subsequent writings that "the sensibility of the left is an intrinsic feature of an authentic theology."[25] However, because no social system is without its defects, there can be no guarantee in advance that socialist experiments in Latin America will bear fruit, anymore than it could be demanded of Jesus that before healing a sick person "he should give a guarantee that the cure will not be followed by an even graver illness."[26] Therefore, although in the end Segundo opts for socialism, it is nonetheless an open-ended version:

[In it] ownership is exercised as much as possible, in true communities—something very different from a useless statism. Any Latin American will admit that everything is not really at the service of everyone unless all can somehow have responsibility for it, thus making it *their own*.[27]

As indicated earlier, one of Segundo's most valuable contributions to Latin American liberation theology is his concern for the relationship between faith and ideology. In his *Faith and Ideologies* he elaborates on this theme, contending that "faith is never faith without ideologies," and that "ideology without faith is never an ideology."[28] He notes, for example, the variety of meanings attached to the term "Marxism." Therefore, one can no more talk about an abstract "Marxist ideology" than one can extrapolate a capitalist ideology. Segundo would prefer to find new terminology that is not so laden with emotion—terminology reflective of the basic concern for Latin Americans to reconstruct their society "from the roots of their relational base up."[29]

Faith and Ideologies is but the first of a five-volume series that could turn out to be one of the stunning theological achievements of the 1980s. This series may do for the liberation theology of this generation what Paul Tillich's writings did for the relationship between theology and culture in the previous generation. Segundo is especially important because he is a Latin American liberation theologian whose fertile and original mind ranges far and wide over a vast spectrum of theological issues. He creates his theological thinking as a response to grass-roots communities while keeping his Christian faith at the very core of his thinking and action.[30]

Rubem Alves

The thinking of Rubem Alves, more than that of most other Latin American liberation theologians, is grounded in the European theology of hope. As I have already suggested, this theology, exemplified particularly in the writings of the German theologians Jürgen Moltmann and Wolfhart Pannenberg, emphasizes the eschatological dimension of history. History in this view is understood as futuristic, open to new beginnings, with God as the promise of eventual fulfillment. For these theologians human salvation is social in character, geared toward social justice and human liberation. God is envisioned as the "power of the future," leading humanity toward the fulfillment of social justice.

Alves's close identification with European political theology has arisen, in part, from his graduate work at Union and Princeton Seminaries in the United States.[31] His first book, *A Theology of Human Hope* (1969), was based on his doctoral dissertation at Princeton University.

Because Alves is very much at home with the writings of Jürgen Moltmann, Juan Segundo has branded him "a disciple of Moltmann."[32] Such a characterization, however, is misleading, for even in his *A Theology of Human Hope* Alves is highly critical of Moltmann, a judgment that becomes increasingly severe in his later writings. In his first book Alves faults Moltmann for focusing almost exclusively on the transcendent dimension of eschatology, thereby giving second place to the human dimension. For Alves, hope is not something transcendent beckoning humanity from beyond; rather, hope is "the stretching out of human consciousness, as it looks beyond the unfinishedness of 'what is.' "[33] Alves advocates what he calls a "political humanism"—that is, a creative, open-ended process that continually affirms that a better tomorrow can be achieved. This political humanism contains three components. First, it denies finality to the present inhuman structures; they by no means represent the final chapter in human history. Secondly, one must always continue to hope that the future will include the elimination of these present oppressive forms. Thirdly, it is humanity and humanity alone that will effect these changes and create new structures that promote human justice. Alves does not contend that the perfect social order can be achieved, but that a far better society than the present can emerge.

For Alves the term "violence" means anything that keeps humans from realizing a better future. In short, violence is the "power of defuturization." Alves makes much of the notion of freedom and even suggests a "language of freedom," entirely secular in nature, which "does not look behind the stars first in order to find a meaning for the earth."[34]

Critics may well ask, Where is God in all this? Alves replies:

[God is] the power for humanization that remains determined to make men historically free even when all objective and subjective possibilities immanent in history have been exhausted. . . . The beginning, middle and end of God's activity is the liberation of men. . . . To speak about God is to speak about the historical events that made and make men free.[35]

Like many of his Latin American counterparts, Alves makes much of the concept of a suffering God. In language reminiscent of German theologian Dietrich Bonhoeffer, Alves suggests that God is to be found among the weak and oppressed: suffering with them, yet hoping with them in the creation of a better future. For Alves, God is not the explantion of suffering, but rather the one whose suffering makes it possible to believe in a better tomorrow. Critics of Alves charge that he rejects any sense of transcendence; for him, God, is but another name for human suffering, hope, and freedom. Even the resurrection becomes for Alves a symbol of human aspirations, not evidence for a transcendent reality. Alves seems to be straining to find language that will reject an either/or and affirm a both/and approach to God. But he must still face the question, Can God operate independently of humanity and can humanity operate independently of God? Do the twain meet—or should Alves admit that they are one and the same?

This ambiguity in Alves's writings becomes even more pronounced in the 1970s as his views become more radicalized. His own story of his theological pilgrimage, as recorded in his article "From Paradise to the Desert: Autobiographical Musings," illustrates this difficulty.[36] In his earlier years he had been a fundamentalist Christian who found a sense of security in the Presbyterian

Church. But he lost his simple faith during his years as a student at Campinas Presbyterian Seminary and found refuge in a community of friends who began to sense the terrible plight of the poor and oppressed, and the apparent indifference of the established churches. Alves left his own church as a protest against its social and political conservatism and directed his attention to the cries of the oppressed for political, economic, and social liberation. He came to see that truth was not a matter of what the church proclaimed:

> Truth is the name given by an historical community to those historical acts which were, are and will be, effective for the liberation of man. Truth is action.[37]

Later still, Alves even called into question the inherent value of the struggle for human liberation, wondering if it is worth the effort. As he puts it:

> Our age-old hopes have not been fulfilled. We live amid the ruins of our religious expectations. Our backs are to the wall and there is no escape. The exodus of which we dreamed earlier has miscarried. Instead we now find ourselves in a situation of exile and captivity.[38]

For Alves, we have reached the stage at which our gods and our heroes are dead. Technology and bureaucracy have simply overwhelmed us. There are no longer any points of reference; there is no reason for a shred of optimism about a better future. Yet even though we realize that our historical hopes will not be fulfilled, we cannot live without hoping. So what are we to do? We must hope against hope:

> Theology is our effort to bring together the petals of our flower that is continuously torn by a world that does not love flowers.[39]

Religion becomes a matter of imagination and dreams that will at least help us to exist in a harsh world devoid of love and justice. Alves proposes a "theology of captivity," which refuses to accept the world on its own terms, yet finally realizes that a new and better world will probably not become a reality. Those of us who do not have dreams are lost.

So what do we have left? Apparently not much. In his *What is Religion?*, Alves answers his own question by suggesting that "religious entities are imaginary entities" and that religious faith is in reality a *"desire* that it be true."[40] In speaking of religion as the fulfillment of a desire, he seems to echo Sigmund Freud's contention that religion is the fulfillment of an illusion. This conclusion has led Alves's critic, George Hunsinger, to suggest that Alves "apparently has nothing better for the world these days than a few choice quotations from Feuerbach and Nietzsche."[41]

If Alves has reached the point where he can say only that "all is vanity and a striving after wind," in fairness to him we should point out that this fatalism is a product of years of agonizing struggle against the forces of oppression in Latin America that seem only to grow stronger.

Leonardo Boff

Leonardo Boff's chief concern has been to develop a christology for Latin American liberation theology.[42] In his *Jesus Christ Liberator: A Critical Christology for Our Time* (1978), Boff suggests five criteria for constructing a suitable christology.[43] First, an indigenous Latin American christology will focus on human need rather than ecclesiastical dogma and structure. Secondly, its orientation will be toward the future, asking what Christ can do for the oppressed. Thirdly, it will be open to dialogue with the world and not be concerned with preserving the religious mentality of the status quo. Fourthly, it will stress the social dimension of the liberating work of Christ, with special attention given to liberation for the poor and oppressed who have no voice in determining their future. And finally, it will have as its foundation a Christ who calls us to correct action (orthopraxis) even more than to correct beliefs (orthodoxy).

Applying these five criteria, the emergent portrait of Jesus is that of one who is the "liberator of the human condition";[44] the one who advocates the kind of radical love that knows no human discrimination; the one who reflects "all that is authentically human";[45] the one completely open to God, who exhorts us to oppose the oppressors of our day as did Christ in his day. Boff's description of the person and role of Jesus is filled with down-to-earth imagery: "being-for-others to the end," "the human being par excellence," the one who for young persons is a "tremendous high," the dissenter, revolutionary, and liberator.[46]

According to Boff, Jesus' intention was not to establish a new church, but to make clear the dominant qualities of a fully human being. Boff betrays his liberal theological leanings by declaring, "It is not those who are Christian who are good, true, and just. Rather the good, the true, and the just are Christians."[47]

For Boff, a christology for Latin America comes down firmly on the side of the poor and downtrodden. To follow Christ in Latin America is to seek to change the existing social structures that support poverty and oppression:

> The theology of liberation of Jesus Christ the Liberator is the pain-filled cry of oppressed Christians. They are knocking on the door of their affluent brothers and sisters, asking for everything and yet for nothing. Indeed all they ask is to be people, to be accepted as persons. All they ask is that they be allowed to fight to regain their captive freedom.[48]

Boff even asserts that violence might be necessary for the sake of socio-political liberation. However, Christians will never initiate physical violence; they will resort to it only when forced by oppressors to do so.

In his subsequent writings Boff notes how the situation in Latin America today has striking parallels with the socio-political situation of Jesus' time. In developing this theme—one that Juan Segundo considers an improper parallel—Boff points out that Palestine, like the countries of Latin America, was a dependent state suffering from external (Roman) control. Jesus confronted this external domination by preaching about the kingdom of God that would usher in a new era of human liberation. Jesus chose to identify himself with the have-nots, defending their rights and promising them a better day when God's purposes would be consummated on this earth.

Unlike Rubem Alves, who considers the resurrection to be the symbol of human aspirations, Boff sees the resurrection as the ultimate victory of God's love, a victory that is as certain for Latin America today as it was for those to whom Jesus preached. Like Alves, Boff sometimes uses the term "captivity" to illustrate the state of the oppressed Christian today. Like Jesus and indeed because of Jesus, we must continue to hope against hope, living a life of disciplined love, continuing to prepare the soil, and sowing the seeds of human liberation. Unlike Alves, however, Boff is much more confident that God's victory will be achieved.

Boff, in a manner similar to that of Gustavo Gutiérrez, is careful to stress that socio-political liberation is not the only form of liberation. Without prayer and meditation, no liberation is truly Christian. Some of Boff's most eloquent writing centers on the devotional side of religion. For example, in his *Way of the Cross—Way of Justice,* he translates his christology into down-to-earth meditations showing how the inner and outer life of the Christian must be inextricably linked. This combination is beautifully illustrated in Boff's meditation on the resurrection:

Wherever an authentically human life is growing in the world,
wherever justice is triumphing over the instincts of domination,
wherever grace is winning out over the power of sin,
wherever human beings are creating more fraternal mediations in their
    social life together,
wherever love is getting the better of selfish interests,
    and wherever hope is resisting the lure of cynicism or despair,
there the process of resurrection
    is being turned into a reality.[49]

Critics of Latin American liberation theology would do well to read Boff's book on Saint Francis, who, Boff believes, is an ideal model for advocates of liberation theology.[50] Though a rich man, Francis became one with the poor, living and identifying with them and their oppression. What makes Francis an important model for us today is his way of life, his renunciation of material wealth, his identification with the poor, and his closeness to and respect for nature. In his *The Lord's Prayer,* Boff uses the imagery of the forward and upward look, conveying attitudes of hope and faith in a God who is near yet also far away.[51]

There is little doubt that Leonardo Boff is one of the most creative and challenging Latin American liberation theologians, one who displays the many-splendored dimensions of a full-blown liberation theology.

Hugo Assmann

Hugo Assmann's advocacy of liberation theology has made him persona non grata in several Latin American countries. Exiled from Brazil, Bolivia, Chile, and Uruguay, he found a place on the faculty of the school of journalism at the University of Costa Rica.[52]

Assmann's greatest strength lies in his ability to synthesize the major themes of Latin American liberation theology. In his best known book, *Theology for a Nomad Church* (1976), he spells out a theology of liberation that has taken shape since Medellín.[53] The starting point is that every human act has a social and political setting and the Christian obligation is to work for a socio-political setting in which everyone can be fully human. None of the "progressivist theologies" of the developed countries—secular theology, death-of-God theology, political theology, theology of hope—has been specific enough to be applied to the Latin American context—nor have the intraecclesiastical reforms of Vatican II, or the Christian-Marxist dialogues in Europe. Assmann quotes with approval José Comblin's assertion, "Any Latin American who has studied in Europe has to undergo detoxification before he can begin to act."[54]

Assmann singles out for special criticism European political theology, especially its failure to appreciate the need to join with the poor in overcoming oppressive political structures. It is all very well for European theologians to talk about the importance of the role of theology in the ongoing political process and the need for Christians to be involved in political change. Latin American theology goes beyond European political theology when it moves from abstractions to partnership with the poor in their revolutionary struggle.

Like Juan Segundo, Assmann sees a new methodology as the key to liberation theology, a methodology grounded in the social sciences. The essential task of theology is to analyze the actual conditions in which persons live, a task that Assmann calls the "sociologization of theology." And when we analyze these conditions, we discover that violence has been institutionalized, as has poverty and oppression. Here is another difference between Latin American theology and its European and North American counterparts—namely, North Atlantic theology has never been sensitive to the institutionalized oppression that permits millions of human beings to remain under the poverty line. Any theology that does not have as its starting point a preference for the poor will ignore their cries and proceed to ask the wrong abstract questions and be satisfied with wrong idealistic answers.

Assmann maintains that the worst temptation for theology is to engage in absolutes. Indeed, even "the Bible, tradition, the magisterium or teaching authority of the Church, history of dogma, and so on" are but secondary sources of truth.[55] Assmann insists that a normative authoritarian theological perspective cannot take precedence over a commitment to the poor and oppressed.

Assmann maintains that Latin American theology, in its insistence on overcoming evil social conditions, must of necessity advocate revolutionary methods and even class struggle. Why? Because this is the only way that a redistribution of goods and a more just social order can become a reality. For Assmann, as for all Latin American liberation theologians, truth is found not in the realm of ideas, but in the realm of action. The criterion for an authentic theology is whether it reflects de facto historical praxis—there is no point in understanding a world of poverty and oppression unless one is also willing and prepared to change it.

In his subsequent writings, Assmann continues to emphasize the need for social revolution. He argues that, inasmuch as there is a variety of social and political systems in Latin America, liberation theology must be pluriform and experimental in order to be relevant. Echoing Rubem Alves, Assmann suggests that a new language may be needed if a "people's version of theology" is to be developed.

Like Leonardo Boff, Assmann stresses the importance of elaborating a new christology for the Latin American situation. He points out, however, that a pure christology is impossible: there can be no agreement on a normative christology as long as social inequalities continue in existence. Any abstract christology based on slogans such as "Christ the alpha and omega" or "Christ acting in the world" should be treated with suspicion. Assmann is aware of criticism directed against Leonardo Boff for his alleged reduction of Jesus to the figure of a socio-political liberator. Such a model of Christ, Assmann admits, will never achieve popularity, especially among those now in power. But any image of Christ that serves only to support the present social and political order is idolatrous. With Boff, Assmann insists that an adequate christology for Latin America must be one that promises a new life for everyone "in the full dimensions of history here and now today."[56]

In grounding both theology and christology in the social context of the oppressed, Assmann sees Marxist analysis as a useful tool, but not as *the* solution. He faults Marxism for its overemphasis on economic factors; in fact, he is critical of any "ism" that can develop into a positivistic determinism eliminating the human dimension of freedom. Curiously, one finds far fewer references to Karl Marx in the writings of Hugo Assmann and most other Latin American liberation theologians than critics of liberation theology would have us believe. And never is Marxism accepted without qualification, but only as a tool of social analysis. To admit that there are unjust class inequalities does not make one a Marxist.

Assmann uses the phrase "epistemological privilege of the poor," a term that Latin American liberation theologians are using with increasing frequency to suggest that the conditions of oppression endured by the poor make them more open to the liberating word of God than are those who stand in the way of liberation. Assmann believes it important to ground one's view of God in a de facto social context, for the word of God is always mediated through social processes. Christianity has too often been warped by false notions of God, notions that support oppression. It is the "epistemological privilege of the poor" that makes it possible for the liberator God to be revealed.

In his article "The Faith of the Poor in Their Struggle with Idols," Assmann illustrates this concept of the "epistemological privilege of the poor" by bringing together brief statements and revolutionary poems written by both celebrated and uncelebrated believers in Latin America. The following selection from the "Nicaraguan Peasant Mass" illuminates the faith of the poor:

> You are the God of the poor,
>   the human, unassuming God,
>   the God who sweats in the street,
>   the God with a weathered countenance.
> That is why I speak to you,
>   as my people speaks,
>   because you are God the laborer,
>   Christ the worker.
>
> You go hand in hand with my people,
>   you struggle in the countryside and the city,
>   you line up there in the camp
>   so that they will pay you your day's wages.
> You eat, scratching there in the park,
>   with Eusebio, Pancho, and Juan José,
>   and you complain about the syrup
>   when they don't put much molasses in it.
>
> I have seen you in a grocery store,
>   sitting on a stand;
>   I have seen you selling lottery tickets,
>   without being ashamed of that job.
> I have seen you in the gas stations,
>   checking the tires on a truck,
>   and even patrolling highways,
>   with leather gloves and overalls.[57]

Hugo Assmann is a Latin American liberation theologian who has suffered political exile in his espousal of the plight of the poor and oppressed. But he is convinced that the poor know more about the world as God intended it to be than does anyone else. This is precisely why Assmann insists that Christians should not hesitate to side with the poor. For, by seeing the world from the epistemological privilege of the poor, Christians will advance not only the liberation of the poor, but their own liberation as well.

José Porfirio Miranda

José Porfirio Miranda is one of the most controversial Latin American liberation theologians.[58] He seems to occupy his own space, having virtually no contact with the church or his theological colleagues. A native of Mexico, Miranda is a leading advocate of Marxism as an essential tool for understanding and changing Latin American society. He has attempted to bring out many affinities between Marxist teachings and biblical faith.

His first book, *Marx and the Bible: A Critique of the Philosophy of Oppression,* put him at the forefront of Latin American biblical exegesis.[59] His basic theme in this study is the positive correlation between Marx and the Bible. Neither will have love without justice, or justice without love. Both affirm that love and justice make no sense apart from the social matrix; both insist that human beings can lose their selfishness for the sake of loving the neighbor; both seek to change the world for the better rather than simply try to understand it; both believe that such a change for the better can indeed take place. Miranda asks:

> Is it more utopian to hope for the transformation of the world through justice than it is to hope for the definite elimination of sin in the world? Is it more utopian to believe in the resurrection of the flesh than in the abolition of all the injustices, enmities and cruelties in the world? . . . In both Marx and the Bible the basis for all thought is this thesis which is the most revolutionary imaginable: Sin and evil are not inherent to humanity and history; they began one day through human work and they can therefore be eliminated.[60]

Miranda takes pains to note the similarities between Marx and the apostle Paul. Both emphasize the totality of evil. Both believe that injustice and sin can be eliminated, because selfishness is a "fallen" condition, not a natural one. Whereas Marx sees injustice and sin as primarily the consequences of an economic system (capitalism), Paul finds them imbedded in earthly principalities and powers.

In his *Being and the Messiah: The Message of St. John,* Miranda stresses his earlier theme that love and justice are also one and the same in the Johannine tradition:

> The defining characteristic of the God of the Bible is the fact that he cannot be known or loved directly; rather, to love God and to know him means to love one's neighbor and to do one's neighbor justice.[61]

Miranda does not suggest, however, that there are no important differences between Marxism and biblical faith. The most obvious difference is, of course, that biblical faith affirms God and God's involvement in human destiny, whereas orthodox Marxist ideology does not. It is instructive to note what Miranda considers to be the defects of doctrinaire Marxism in its denial of the biblical God:

> In Marxist communism, there can be no justification for care of the old, the mentally retarded, the born cripples. The god known as productivity

has no place for them in the world. How sad that precisely when the human being is really at stake the Marxist foundations are inadequate. Marx's effort, to provide "to each according to his needs" and not according to his productivity is to be applauded, but the limitation of present-day Marxism offers no philosophical basis for such provision. . . .What he [Marx] failed to see is that providing for each according to his needs presupposes caring for people simply because they exist, which in turn presupposes an absolute imperative unknown in his system of thought.[62]

Miranda is not a Marxist ideologue, accepting without question the gospel of Karl Marx and Marx's self-proclaimed, latter-day disciples. Miranda is first and foremost a Christian who is as critical of Marxists and their views of Marx as he is of Christians and their interpretations of Christ. One of Miranda's most helpful insights lies in his condemnation of Marxists who distort the teachings of Marx, a theme that he develops in his book *Marx against the Marxists: The Christian Humanism of Karl Marx*. Here he bluntly affirms:

It is not just the satanic image of Marx concocted by conservatives that is demonstrably false. Equally false is the image of Marx presented by certain revolutionaries who call themselves Marxists.[63]

In this work Miranda turns to Marx's own writings to find out what Marx really taught. He begins by pointing out that, for Marx, the motives for building a more just social order are primarily moral, not materialistic. It simply is not humane that human beings be kept in oppression. Miranda argues that, for Marx, freedom is the essence of humanity, including freedom from socio-economic and political oppression. Marx even suggested that democracy in the United States was "the highest form of political freedom as yet attained in history."[64] Miranda insists that Marx's espousal of determinism never meant that he denied the reality of human freedom. Marx's determinism is basically economic, but "Marx himself never made the absurd claim that all the factors or causes which alter that base are economic."[65]

Miranda concludes that Marx was himself a humanist and that the foundation of humanism "is unlimited respect for the person as an end in himself or herself."[66] It is for this reason that Marx opposed the capitalist system, which he believed treated persons not as ends in themselves but as means to the achievement of profit for the privileged few. The dramatic disparities between the lives of the rich and the poor that Marx both witnessed and experienced in Victorian England contributed to the development of his humanistic philosophy.

Miranda even suggests that because Marx, as a humanist, believed in a moral imperative as basic to the elimination of social injustices, one can note a strong parallel here between Marx's moral imperative and the Christian understanding of God's moral character. According to Miranda, Marx felt a close affinity with the radical social message of Jesus. Marx's basic problem with Christianity was his contention that the followers of Jesus had distorted his teachings—just as later disciples of Marx have, in Miranda's view, perverted the teachings of Marx. Marx often said that early Christianity was socialistic in nature and that he considered his advocacy of communism as an extension of the message of Jesus. Marx also underscored a parallel between his own position and the basic Christian contention that history has a goal, that good will triumph over evil, and that the final consummation will occur on this earth. Miranda concludes that Marx's profession of atheism in his later years should be understood more as a refutation of "Churchianity" than as a denial of the moral idealism of Jesus, which affirmed the final realization of a just social order.

In Miranda's small volume entitled *Communism in the Bible,* we find a vigorous defense of "Christian communism." Miranda considers this book to be his biblical manifesto, which proclaims:

> The notion of communism is in the New Testament right down to the letter—and so well put that in the twenty centuries since it was written no one has come up with a better definition of communism than Luke in Acts 2:44–45 and 4:32–35. In fact, the definition Marx borrowed from Louis Blanc, "From each one according to his capacities, to each one according to his needs," is inspired by, if not directly copied from, Luke's formulation eighteen centuries earlier. There is no clearer demonstration of the brainwashing to which the establishment keeps us subjected than the officially promulgated conception of Christianity as anticommunist.[67]

Miranda believes that most Christians who claim to be anti-Marx have probably never read much of Marx's own writings. He points out, as he did in *Marx against the Marxists,* that communism does not have to be identified with pure materialism, and that Russian communism is not a norm, but, rather, a failure. Miranda's list of common misconceptions about communism is instructive; it includes:

> identifying communism with materialism and atheism, accusing us of chasing mode and fashion, imputing to us a lack of spirituality, alleging we care more for human beings than for God, and attributing to us a greater preoccupation with structures than with persons. It is time to drop all these side issues and concentrate on the fundamental fact: the Bible teaches communism.[68]

Miranda focuses his attention on the early Christian community and reminds us that the early Christians held everything in common, to be distributed according to need (Acts 2:44–45). Renunciation of private property was for Jesus a condition for entering the kingdom (Mark 10:21, 25). Only the poor can enter the kingdom (Luke 6:20). Jesus filled the hungry with good things and sent away the rich (Luke 6:20, 24). You cannot serve God and money (Matt. 6:24).

For Miranda, the choice is between capitalism and communism. In the former, a small minority seeks to impose its will on the rest of the population, keeping for itself a disproportionately large share of the financial resources. In the latter, a large majority seeks to control financial resources in a more equitable manner. A clear choice has to be made between these two systems. There is no third way. Miranda opts for communism because the capitalist system exploits the majority for the sake of a small minority. And the struggle for a just society for everyone is not a preferential option; it is a serious obligation. Miranda insists:

> To the extent that one does not participate in this revolutionary struggle, one participates in the benefits of a society which . . . lives essentially by exploiting and oppressing the poor.[69]

Miranda has been strongly criticized for his sympathetic interpretation of Marx, for ambiguities in his analysis, and for his overeagerness to make Marxism and Christianity compatible. Alfredo Fierro argues that Miranda's Marx is one "Marx himself never wanted to be . . . a Marxism that one can scarcely recognize at all."[70] Nicholas Lash contends that Miranda's reading of the Bible is "tendentious," as is his reading of Marx.[71] Arthur McGovern suggests that Miranda's biblical exegesis is "one-sided" and that he "often does impose a Marxist framework on the Bible."[72] Perhaps the most widespread criticism of Miranda is that, within his writings, there is an implied inference that he has discovered the correct interpretation of scripture—a charge that is also leveled against his interpretation of Marx.

In fairness, however, it should be pointed out, once again, that Miranda is not an ideologue who simply bends and twists both Christianity and Marxism to make them fit together. Miranda is highly critical of many components of Marxist ideology; yet he is not afraid to see the positive features in Marxism and the resemblance they bear to many basic biblical insights. Miranda is justified in criticizing those anti-Marxists who have never bothered to read Marx, but who have settled for a passing acquaintance with Marx through the sometimes distorted lenses of some of his antagonists. What is crucial to stress here is that the Marxist component one finds in some, but not all, Latin American liberation theology cannot be fairly and fully appreciated until one is willing to come to terms with José Miranda.

By no means should we minimize Miranda's own deep Christian faith. He affirms again and again that one really believes in Jesus Christ only if one also believes that this world can be changed for the better and that the kingdom of God can be realized on this earth. For Miranda the bottom line is that to do justice—"to preach good news to the poor . . . to set at liberty those who are oppressed"—is to follow Christ and to know God.

José Míguez Bonino

José Míguez Bonino and Rubem Alves are among the very few Protestant liberation theologians in an overwhelmingly Catholic Latin America. The interests of these two theologians, however, are quite different. As noted above, Alves's ties to the church have weakened through the years as he came to advocate a "theology of captivity" centering on dreams that will protect humanity from the harsh realities of the real world. Míguez Bonino continues as an active Methodist clergyman who has served as a president of the World Council of Churches.[73]

The author of several books, Míguez Bonino's major contribution to the development of liberation theology is his *Doing Theology in a Revolutionary Situation*.[74] This book serves as an excellent introduction to the main features of Latin American theology, particularly the conviction that theology must emerge out of the lives of the oppressed in their own encounter with the biblical texts, a process that Míguez Bonino calls "hermeneutical circulation." He traces the development of what he calls a "new breed of Christians" in Latin America, focusing on the Christians for Socialism conference in Santiago, Chile, as pivotal in this development. This book is also helpful in its treatment of some of the major agreements and differences among some liberation theologians.

In his writings, Míguez Bonino devotes considerable attention to the capitalism-socialism debate. He faults the capitalist system for its profit-motive basis (which in Latin America has resulted in the dehumanization of large sectors of the population) and its apparent indifference to the plight of the poor. These glaring inequalities will continue to exist as long as economic dependence on outside powers continues. In a manner reminiscent of Gustavo Gutiérrez and Juan Segundo, Míguez Bonino suggests a new form of socialism that would eliminate the basic inequalities of the capitalist system yet not be a mere parroting of doctrinaire Marxism. He takes pains to point out that Latin American liberation theologians are not socialist ideologues fomenting radical social change. Rather, they are committed Christians seeking to forge a new society of liberated human beings. They have become social activists *because* of their Christian faith, not because of Marxist ideology. But they have learned that Marxist analysis is helpful in understanding and correcting social inequalities. In words echoing José Miranda, Míguez Bonino points out that Marxist analysis "teaches us to see class struggle, not as a general consequence of sin, nor as a deplorable accident, but—as Calvin himself saw—as a war prompted by greed and power."[75]

For the Christian community this means that what is at stake is not a specifically *Christian* struggle, but basically a *human* struggle of the oppressed against oppressors. And Christians, like everyone else interested in social analysis, need to use the best available tools, including Marxist thought. If at some point revolution and even violence become necessary for the oppressed to receive their due, it is not because of any Marxist dogma, but because the violence of oppressors demands it.

Míguez Bonino joins Gustavo Gutiérrez, Juan Segundo, Rubem Alves, and other liberation theologians in criticizing Jürgen Moltmann and other European theologians for advocating a "critical theory" that claims to remain above all theologies and ideologies as a kind of all-encompassing judge. Such a neutral stance, Míguez Bonino insists, is impossible:

> There is no *divine* politics or economics. But this means that we must resolutely use the best *human* politics and economics at our disposal.[76]

But he also warns against the tendency among some Latin American liberation theologians to equate Christianity with a specific social program. He calls this tendency the "radical 'monism' of the new liberation theology," a view that makes the love of God and of neighbor one and the same.[77] Such a stance would lead to "unwittingly deifying [the] history of humanity. . . . In that case we would do better to call things by their right name and profess to total immanentism."[78]

Míguez Bonino seeks to tread the difficult line between the general and the specific, between the "critical theory" stance and the radical "monism" tendency. He believes it important, for example, to use Marxist insights without becoming, or being thought to be, a thoroughgoing Marxist. Nonetheless, he is convinced of the importance of revolutionary change. In his *Christians and Marxists: The Mutual Challenge to Revolution,* he writes:

> As a Latin American Christian I am convinced . . . that revolutionary action aimed at changing the basic economic, political, social and cultural structures and conditions of life is imperative today in the world. Ours is not a time for mere development, rearranging or correction, but for basic revolutionary change (which ought not to be equated necessarily with violence) . . . the sociological tools, the historical horizon of interpretation, the insights into the dynamics of the social process and the revolutionary ethos and programme which Marxism has either received and appropriated or itself created are, however corrected or interpreted, indispensable for revolutionary change.[79]

Míguez Bonino points out that, until recently, Christianity and Marxism had been considered inherently contradictory. Only in recent years has there been a major attempt on the part of some Christians and Marxists to find common ground. He attributes this change both to the failure of capitalism to remedy the glaring inequalities of the social order and to the emergence of a more open-ended Marxism. He applauds this new rapprochement and argues that if Marx is right in his contention that religion has often been "the opiate of the people," then Christians should willingly accept this criticism and revise their view of religion accordingly. On the other hand, Christians should never hesitate to expunge the elements in Marxist thought that are alien to the Christian affirmation of the ultimacy of love.

In an article, "For Life against Death: A Theology that Takes Sides," Míguez Bonino confronts Marxism head-on:

> I have never felt attracted to Marxism as a system, neither have I felt inclined to enroll in any anti-Marxist crusade. . . . I have more and more come to think in terms of a long humanist-socialist tradition, with early Christian and Hellenic roots which have developed in the modern world, in which Marx has played an insistent—even decisive—part, but which he has neither created nor fulfilled.[80]

Why should we not work with Marxists on matters of mutual benefit? Why should we not join forces with all persons of good will who seek for a world of justice and freedom for all? Let us "demythologize" the Marx question once and for all!

Two other books show how Míguez Bonino's thought continues to develop. In *Faces of Jesus: Latin American Christologies,* of which he is the editor, he gathers together a collection of essays directed toward the emergence of an adequate christology for Latin America.[81] Here we find images of Christ that bear a strong resemblance to Leonardo Boff's portraits of Christ: Christ of oppression, Christ who conquers death, the revolutionary Christ, and so on. In his *Toward a Christian Political Ethics,* Míguez Bonino carves out a political ethic for Latin America with liberation as the key ingredient.[82] Here he analyzes the development of Christian political ethics from the arrival of Spaniards on Latin American soil to the present day when we "sowed modern democracy and reaped the national security state."[83] He contends that the basic ethical problem for Latin America today is how to maximize universal human possibilities while minimizing human cost.

Míguez Bonino is especially important both for his concern to develop a Christian political ethic for Latin America and for his contribution to the Christian-Marxist dialogue.

Jon Sobrino

Jon Sobrino joins Leonardo Boff in making his major contribution the development of a christology appropriate for the Latin American setting.[84] In his *Christology at the Crossroads: A Latin American Approach,* Sobrino agrees with Boff in pointing to the close parallel between the contemporary Latin American setting and the historical context in which Jesus lived.[85]

Sobrino finds traditional views on the nature of Christ devoid of historical and grass-roots relevance. He calls them "Christologies of descent," because they try to superimpose on any given cultural setting a prepackaged, abstract scheme of salvation.[86] These classic views begin with the dogmatic claim that God became human in Christ, and then proceed to spell out the general implications of this divine act for all humankind. Little wonder, then, that these christologies appear "historically alienating and open to manipulation, completely lacking in human relevance."[87] Sobrino contends that the starting point for christology should be "the underside of history," an idea that has increasingly gained favor among Latin American liberation theologians. By this term Sobrino means that one should begin with the actual events of the lives of oppressed peoples and of a Jesus who is himself rooted in a particular history. From this perspective we should ask, What does Jesus mean by the kingdom of God? If we begin this way, we discover:

> Jesus calls attention to the coexistence of oppressor and oppressed, insisting that such a situation is the result of human free will rather than something willed or even permitted by God. Denouncing the situation in the prophetic manner, Jesus says there is poverty because the rich will not share their wealth, ignorance because the learned have stolen away the keys to knowledge, and oppression because the Pharisees have imposed intolerable burdens on people, and rulers are acting despotically.[88]

The kingdom of God becomes the building of a new life in which God is not understood as an addition to life, but the full affirmation of life itself. Sobrino sees in Jesus' resurrection a radical openness to the future possibility that this kingdom can be realized.

For Sobrino, the resurrection is not a once-and-for-all event of the past, but an ongoing "faith against unbelief, a hope against hope, and a love against alienation."[89] Sobrino wants to hold together the dimensions of transcendence and immanence, for he believes that the temptation on the part of classic christologies has been to dwell on the transcendent at the expense of the historical. Sobrino insists that a commitment to the historical must be primary.

Sobrino's discussion of christology ranges far and wide over historical and contemporary views of Christ, including an exposition of the "European christologies" of Rahner, Pannenburg, and Moltmann. In fourteen succinct theses he shows how his views differ from theirs and from those of earlier classic theologians. Like Rubem Alves, Sobrino makes much of the notion of a suffering God, one who, by entering into the struggle for human liberation in the person of Jesus, takes on the hurts of history, including the devastating pain so evident in the crucifixion. As God's disciples, we are called to identify with God's suffering by becoming involved ourselves at precisely those historical conjunctures that deny God's sovereignty—that is, those times and places where human oppression is affirmed and human liberation is denied.

Jon Sobrino's *Christology at the Crossroads* is an important addition to the small but growing literature among Latin American theologians that seeks to develop an authentic christology for the poor and oppressed. One might add that Marx appears only once in the book.

Sobrino does make extensive reference to Karl Marx, however, in his important article "Theological Understanding in the Theology of Europe and Latin

America."[90] Here he contrasts the views of European theologians who ground their views in the Enlightenment—especially in the thought of Immanuel Kant who advocated the liberation of human reason from divine authority—with contemporary Latin American liberation theologians who look to Karl Marx as the liberator from the authority of social oppressors. The goals of the two approaches are markedly different. The former sought above all to *understand* reality through human reason; the latter's primary concern was to *transform* reality through social action. Sobrino obviously aligns himself with the latter approach:

> To know the truth is to do the truth, to know Jesus is to follow Jesus, to know sin is to take on the burden of sin, to know suffering is to free the world from suffering, to know God is to go to God in justice.[91]

In other writings Sobrino develops the notion of the church as the extension of Christ's liberating action. The role of the church is to bear witness to life in behalf of justice and liberation, especially those facets of life now being destroyed by institutionalized violence and injustice. In short, to bear witness to God in Christ is to affirm a life of justice and liberation. This affirmation must include in particular the economic, social, and political dimensions—in Sobrino's phrase, "the ongoing humanization of the human realm."[92] This coalescence of "humanization and Christianization" continues as a major theme in Sobrino's writings, a theme that he and Leonardo Boff vigorously defend. If the church fails to lead in this process of humanization, it fails Christ.

In another important article, "The Epiphany of the God of Life in Jesus of Nazareth," Sobrino uses bread as the symbol of the new life in the church and in Christ.[93] The bread of life has both a physical and spiritual component. How, then, can one receive the bread of life in a full Christian sense if one is literally starving physically? The absence of this bread is the absence of God and is caused, not by God's unwillingness to be present, but by selfish human beings who use their power to keep this bread from those who need it. This need for the bread of life becomes the battleground between the true God and the false gods who are invoked by oppressors to keep the oppressed in their place. This is the reason why Jesus' understanding of God as the giver of the bread of life is so radically opposed by the powerful who do not want to relinquish their privileged status. It is not surprising, then, that to follow Jesus is to cause division between the rich and the poor.

One critic, Dennis McCann, has reproved Sobrino for his failure to stress the notion of conscientization, so crucial to the views of Gutiérrez, Segundo, and others. This omission even leads McCann to suggest that Sobrino is not really a true advocate of liberation theology, and that his *Christology at the Crossroads* is but another form of European theology whose only "distinctly Latin American" aspect is that "its author [born in Spain] happens to teach in El Salvador."[94]

It is difficult, however, to see any justification for this criticism. To be sure, Sobrino does not make much use of the term "conscientization," and both Sobrino and Leonardo Boff have made extensive use of the writings of leading European theologians, prompting critics to charge that they are more European than Latin American in their christological views. But familiarity with the views of others hardly means agreement; both writers make quite clear their disagreements with European thinkers. Also, just because Sobrino does not dwell on the term "conscientization" does not mean that he neglects the importance of that concept. Quite the contrary. Sobrino's basic notion of human liberation includes reeducation, reappropriation, and reaffirmation on the part of the oppressed. Therefore, to call Sobrino a European theologian in disguise, because he makes little of conscientization, is as unfair as to say that Rubem Alves is but a disciple of Moltmann or that Juan Segundo, because he seems to dwell more on methodology than on christology, is not really a liberation theologian. Latin American liberation theologians have developed certain basic features that are crucial to their understanding of liberation theology, a point that should underscore the contention that liberation theology is not monolithic but, like other types of theology, richly varied.

Sobrino's overriding concern is to make Christ come alive in the context of Latin American oppression. This point is well expressed in his response to the murder of the four churchwomen in El Salvador in 1980:

> Maura, Ita, Dorothy, and Jean are Christ dead today. But they are also the Risen Christ, who keeps alive the hope of liberation. Their assassination has affected the entire world and moved it to indignation. But to Christians, this assassination also speaks to us of God, because these women say something to us about God. . . . Salvation comes to us through all men and women who love truth rather than falsehood, who are more disposed to give rather than receive, whose greatest love is giving their life rather than keeping it for themselves. This is where God makes himself present.[95]

José Comblin

A common characteristic of Latin American liberation theologians is their effort to combine political activism with a deep concern for the devotional life. A splendid example is José Comblin.[96] The author of over twenty books, Comblin assumes the role of acute political analyst in his *The Church and the National Security State.*[97] In this study he defends the role of the church as a political agent in support of the underprivileged and their determination to build a just society. Tracing the various historical stages of the colonial/neocolonial systems that have held Latin America in servitude—the Spanish-Portuguese, the British, and the North American—Comblin finds the last one, epitomized by the Pentagon and the Central Intelligence Agency, the most violent. According to Comblin, these agencies have spared no effort in perpetuating military dictatorships, consolidating American financial interests, and inhibiting human rights under the guise of an unbridled war against communism. Comblin points out that the militancy of many Latin American liberation theologians derives from their experience of the ruthlessness of the support that the CIA and the Pentagon lend to oppressive social structures.

Comblin acknowledges the value of Marxist analysis in bolstering the efforts of the underprivileged to achieve justice. But at the same time he does not hesitate to condemn the kind of Marxist practice in which the political system seeks power at the expense of individual freedom:

> In Marxist revolution there is no freedom for the people, only for the party. The same science that expels freedom from history and revolution expels God from humankind and history. The party is supposed to be sufficient to create a new world, but it ends by creating a new power.[98]

Comblin believes it incumbent upon theologians to develop a theology of revolution that will take into account the deepest longings of human existence in the building of a just and free society, a society in which everyone has a responsibility in the shaping of a new people.

Like all other Latin American liberation theologians, Comblin sees the base ecclesial communities as the seedbed for a theology of revolution. But he does not advocate violence. No liberation theologian prefers violence, he argues, but there are times when one faces the unavoidable situation of choosing between no action, which condones the violence of oppressors, and action that may risk fomenting violence. This is never an easy choice and is the kind of decision that Comblin believes is sanctioned by the Catholic notion of the "just war."

Comblin's own strong commitment to the life of devotion can be noted in his books *Sent from the Father: Meditations on the Fourth Gospel;*[99] *Jesus of Nazareth: Meditations on His Humanity;*[100] *The Meaning of Mission: Jesus, Christians, and the Wayfaring Church.*[101] In the last-named work he contrasts two ways in which mission can be understood. Here his analysis is reminiscent of the views of Leonardo Boff and Hugo Assmann. The first and traditional way operates from within the church, seeking visible, quantitative results and a uniformity of belief and practice. The other way, which Comblin advocates, has its starting point outside the church and has, as its goal, the transformation of lives and the encouragement of diversity. Individuals are more important than church structures. From this perspective salvation is not something that is handed out from missionaries to converts. Rather, salvation begins and ends in the life of the individual and combines both a mystical and political dimension. In Comblin's words:

> It is political because we live enslaved to oppressive structures from which we must free ourselves in order to establish justice. It is mystical because this effort would turn into another form of oppression if it were not motivated by, and suffused with, human freedom and love.[102]

One point noted by critics is that Comblin's theological views remain conservative and are seemingly untouched by his radical position on social issues and his reformist attitude toward the mission and structure of the church. He has contended that liberation theology does not "alter the traditional content of biblical revelation. It does not threaten God, Christ, the church, the sacraments, prayer, dogmas, moral theology, or ecclesiastical institutions."[103] This rather static view of theology is reaffirmed in Comblin's conviction that the fundamental issue for liberation theology "is of a practical nature rather than a theological nature."[104] This again is but another example of theological diversity among Latin American theologians. Comblin's great achievement remains his twin commitment to revolutionary praxis and the devotional life.

Enrique Dussel

Enrique Dussel has made his mark primarily as a church historian.[105] President of the Commission on the Study of the History of the Church in Latin America, Dussel's major study is *A History of the Church in Latin America: Colonialism to Liberation*. Míguez Bonino refers to this book as "the best conceived and realized one-volume history of the Church in Latin America."[106]

In his writings Dussel comes across more as an interpreter and synthesizer of the main features of Latin American liberation theology than as an original thinker. For example, he is critical of the European "theology of hope" for its failure to seriously take into account indigenous economic and political factors. In so doing it "has disemboweled hope and even turned it into opium."[107] He favors socialism over capitalism, but a socialism that need not be Marxist. For Dussel, the original sin in Latin America has been colonial domination based on capitalism. But he faults Marxism for its failure to affirm the Other, which leaves it with a closed system lacking a transcendent reference with which to critique itself. Dussel agrees with Míguez Bonino in preferring the term "people" to "class" in describing the oppressed. Although the term "people" is admittedly ambiguous, it does go beyond class distinction to encompass grassroots communities in their political, economic, and cultural dimensions, a people who must play a leading role in its own liberation.[108]

Dussel also argues that we must recover the analogical dimension of Catholic theology. According to Dussel, the problem with traditional theology is that it universalized a particular European theology and abstractly superimposed it on Latin America, Africa, and Asia. Dussel argues that the Third World must be free to develop its own distinctive methodologies and theologies, while participating analogically in Christ's universal church. Dussel believes that the universalization of the particular is idolatrous, for it amounts to a denial of the Other. Acceptance of the Other relativizes all particular systems. To be sure, theology must be historically grounded, but we must beware of absolutizing the finite, whether it be in Europe or Latin America. Analogically speaking, only the Other can be absolutized; in this sense Dussel can insist that there is only one theology.

But Christians must also be "atheists of the fetish"—that is, they must be critical of all human systems.[109] For Dussel the only authentic criterion for judging whether we are truly on the side of God is whether "we struggle unto death for the poor. That is an objective, concrete Christological criticism: 'I was hungry; you gave me to eat.' "

Like so many of his Latin American colleagues, Dussel points to idolatry as a critical problem for Christians: believing in false gods only lulls one into somnolent complacency and an acceptance of the status quo. For Dussel and his colleagues the only way to escape from idolatry is to show a preference for the liberation of the poor. To put it another way, the death of God means in reality "the death of the other human being."

Atheism in itself is not the problem; for when one claims to be an atheist, the question should be asked, Atheism with respect to what conceptualization of God? Chances are that the answer to that question would reveal many Christian atheists among the poor and oppressed!

With respect to the kingdom of God, Dussel uses the terms "not yet" and "already" to indicate that in Jesus the kingdom has in one sense already come, but in another sense is "not yet"—until the poor become liberated human beings:

> If there were no poor, then either we would be "already" in a Kingdom without any "not yet" or would be in an idolatrous Kingdom of this world.[110]

In his deep sensitivity to the plight of the poor, Enrique Dussel reveals his principal concern, a concern that is in no way compromised by his scholarly skills as a church historian.

THEMATIC DIVERSITY AND RICHNESS

The Latin American liberation theologians whom we have covered thus far can all be considered major figures. But others could just as well be included in this category. The intention in this section is to highlight the thinking of certain individuals whose writings are not only influential but representative of the rich diversity of Latin American liberation theology.

Segundo Galilea

Segundo Galilea makes a strong case for theological pluralism.[111] He notes that, although Latin American liberation theologians agree on the undeniable sinful facts of underdevelopment, oppression, and injustice that pervade Latin America, they disagree on nearly everything else. Galilea is particularly sensitive to the charge that Marxism and blatant politicism are necessary ingredients of liberation theology. He insists that no serious liberation theologian is guilty of such a charge: every one of them makes evangelization, not politics, the starting point of theology. But, of course, those who evangelize must be sensitive to the cultural context; one does not evangelize in a vacuum. Authentic evangelization must be cognizant of the popular religion and cultural identity of those whom they want to help to achieve liberation. In the past, mission work has too often included the imposition of foreign cultural baggage. For example, most of the early missionaries linked their faith with their Iberian culture; theirs was a "church made from the top down." But if this process can be reversed, Galilea believes that more and more Latin Americans will choose to identify with the church, and in this process of social and political transformation the church also will change.

Following Gustavo Gutiérrez, José Comblin, and others, Galilea points to the need for a "liberation spirituality," a theme that he develops in his book *Following Jesus*.[112] Here he argues that authentic liberation must unite the mystic with the militant, the contemplative with the politician. For Galilea, true contemplation does not mean a withdrawal from the world of action. Quite the opposite. It means experiencing the presence of God as we encounter our neighbor in the world of action. To be sure, there is always the risk of politicizing the gospel as we seek for God in the here and now, but this danger must never keep us from affirming the political dimension of the gospel. The continuing challenge for Christians is to avoid the two extremes: an introverted Christ devoid of socio-political involvement and a revolutionary Christ engaged exclusively in political agitation. Galilea makes an important contribution to liberation theology in his view of Jesus who, although not advocating a specific political program, did insist that the gospel has profound social and political implications for the lives of the poor.

Ernesto Cardenal

Ernesto Cardenal is a splendid example of the poet become politician. Minister of culture in the revolutionary government of Nicaragua, he previously ministered to the community of Solentiname, a group of about two thousand persons in a remote archipelago on Lake Nicaragua. There he and the community engaged in a continuing series of dialogues that related the gospel lesson of the daily Mass to their everyday lives. Over a hundred of these dialogues, taking place over a period of ten years, have been published in the four-volume series *The Gospel in Solentiname*.[113] This "people's church" is the very stuff out of which liberation theology has emerged.

When the Solentiname community was destroyed by the Nicaraguan National Guard in the late 1970s, Cardenal gradually renounced his pacifism, which had been nurtured by Thomas Merton at the Gethsemene Trappist monastery in Kentucky twenty years earlier. He cast his lot with the revolutionaries seeking to overthrow the dictatorial Somoza government. When the Sandinistas succeeded in their struggle, the poet became the politician and remained very much involved in the Nicaraguan struggle for social justice.[114] He looks forward, however, to the day when the poet in him can return to the Solentiname community.

Antonio Pérez-Esclarín

Antonio Pérez-Esclarín sees the chief contribution of Latin American liberation theology in the fresh meaning it gives to the conception of God as liberator.[115] With other liberation theologians he contends that idolatry is worse than atheism, a theme that he explores in his book *Atheism and Liberation*.[116] Of the idolatrous God in which oppressors believe, he writes:

> [It] is the God of the white conqueror, the God who expects submission from those who are enslaved . . . the God of the colonizers who denies humanity and equality to the colonized.[117]

Far better to be an atheist than to believe in that kind of God!

Pérez-Esclarín contends that the true God's incarnation in Jesus gives us a living embodiment of the concrete meaning of liberation, a point that he develops in his modern parable *Jesus of Gramoven*.[118] In this narrative, he relates the story of Jesús Rodríguez, a resident of the slums of Caracas, through the course of Holy Week. In the end he is kidnapped as a "communist activist" and disappears from history.

J. B. Libânio

J. B. Libânio is another liberation theologian who weaves together the political and spiritual components of the liberated life.[119] In *Spiritual Discernment and Politics: Guidelines for Religious Communities*, he illuminates the close relationship between politics and scripture, identifying a form of praxis that he calls "spiritual discernment."[120] For Libânio, every religious act has political significance, particularly for the poor, who are the principal bearers of the gospel.

José Severino Croatto

José Severino Croatto's great strength lies in his espousal of a biblical hermeneutic for Latin America.[121] He insists that there can be no definitive biblical hermeneutic (or closed christology), because the different historical accumulations of meaning require ever renewed reinterpretation. He is adamant on this point:

> The theology of the Third World has burst upon the scene with a hermeneutic challenge. Like the theology that is arising in the world of the poor, all theologies of liberation (socio-political, religious, women's, black, "theologic" and so on) mean to decipher a liberating God's new manifestation in situations of injustice and alienation. For, in the suffering of the poor, we are assisting at a new God-event. The poor are raising their consciousness and fighting for liberation. It is they, first and fore-

most, who "recognize" God, and who pronounce the first "word"—the first interpretation—of the God-event.[122]

Croatto also dwells on the unending struggle between Yahweh and "oppressor gods," and asserts that, in a real sense the theme of the entire Bible is "the battle of the gods."[123]

He is also one of a growing cadre of liberation theologians intent on developing an authentic christology for Latin America. Like Leonardo Boff, he portrays Jesus as "the one who reveals human values," the one who seeks out the oppressed, the one who knows firsthand what it means to be marginalized and denounced by oppressors.

Like many other liberation theologians, Croatto finds strong parallels between the experiences of the early Christians and those of the oppressed peoples of the Third World.

Elsa Tamez

Elsa Tamez is another liberation theologian intent on developing a biblical hermeneutic that focuses on the Latin American oppressed.[124] In *Bible of the Oppressed* she presents a powerful exposition of the biblical theme of oppressed versus oppressor and its relevance for Latin America.[125] She sees the biblical drama as a continuing struggle on the part of the poor against the rich and comfortable—a theme that she does not find in European and North American forms of biblical theology.

Tamez is one of the very few Latin American liberation theologians who makes extensive use of the writings of José Miranda. She is also one of the very few who point to sexism as a major form of oppression. She uses the biblical story of Hagar as an example of a woman who suffered oppression for three reasons: class, race, and sex. In a modern exposition of the Magnificat (Luke 1:46–55), Tamez ends by addressing God:

> You have created us black, brown, yellow, white and red; male and female. We praise you because, in the midst of oppression, trials, tribulations, pain and injustice—caused by sinful human beings—you reign as our Sustainer. As in the resurrection of Jesus Christ, you have shown us that suffering is not the end but that you are the supreme and final liberator.[126]

Otto Maduro

Otto Maduro is an avowed Christian Marxist who admits that Marx's social analysis must be radically reinterpreted for the Latin American context.[127] In *Religion and Social Conflicts* he provides a critical social analysis of religion, arguing that the social function of a religion will vary according to the needs of a particular society.[128] Heretofore, most sociology of religion emanating from

Latin America has been done from a European perspective, thus suffering the same fate as imported European theology. Maduro argues that there is no such thing as "the social function of religion in general"; Latin American social theorists in each country must develop a *"Latin American praxis of the socialist self-liberation of the oppressed."*[129]

Maduro belongs to the large group of Latin American liberation theologians—Juan Segundo, Míguez Bonino, Hugo Assmann, Gustavo Gutiérrez, José Miranda—willing to incorporate Marxist insights, but only in a greatly modified form.

Noel Leo Erskine

Noel Erskine is important for relating liberation theology to the Caribbean context.[130] A native of Jamaica, Erskine is much more sensitive to racism than are his Latin American counterparts. In *Decolonizing Theology: A Caribbean Perspective*, he develops the theme that, just as the Caribbean has been wrongly interpreted from a First World perspective, so too would it be incorrectly analyzed "through Latin American lenses."[131] Erskine traces the unique history of the colonization of Jamaica, which involved the importation of Africans as slaves, and points out how the black experience of slavery in Jamaica differs from slavery in the context of North America.

For Erskine, the "decolonizing" of theology must recognize a powerful racial component that goes beyond socio-economic factors and class distinctions. Liberation from economic oppression is only part of the task. Integral freedom must be the goal of liberation.

Beatriz Melano Couch

Like Erskine, Beatriz Melano Couch is a Protestant theologian whose understanding of oppression transcends socio-economic factors to include, in her case, sexism.[132] Couch's important contribution is her development of a new hermeneutic, a "hermeneutic of suspicion," that warns us against thinking that our ideas and perceptions can ever be free from prejudice. This element of suspicion, if taken seriously, should lead to a "hermeneutic of hope"—hope that a more candid knowledge of a particular social setting will lead to a more accurate reading of sacred scripture. In turn, this sense of hope should give way to a "hermeneutic of engagement" in which we commit ourselves to overcoming the evils of oppression.[133] Engagement is essential, for it is illusory to think that one can remain neutral. Either we become allies of the oppressed or by default we become friends of oppressors.

Couch sees herself not as a feminist theologian but as a liberation theologian "working with men in both dialogue and struggle on the road together."[134]

Thomas Hanks

Thomas Hanks is a good example of an evangelical theologian who has become a strong advocate of liberation theology. A graduate of Wheaton

Graduate School of Theology, Hanks went to Costa Rica in 1963 as a representative of Inter-varsity and while there became transformed by his exposure to poverty and oppression. His *God So Loved the Third World: The Biblical Vocabulary of Oppression* is biblical exegesis from an evangelical perspective, but with a decidedly liberationist bent.[135] For this reason the book is of particular importance for evangelical Christians who, Hanks insists, often unfairly caricature Latin American liberation theology as sanctioning violence. Hanks argues:

> Pacifism is much more dominant in Latin American theology in praxis than in the U.S.A., where clergy can bless napalm for Vietnam, call for neutron bombs in Europe, and sing 'Onward Christian Soldiers' whenever the marines invade—without providing even a raised eyebrow in most circles.[136]

He concludes with a personal testimony:

> Opportunities for service in a reformatory, literacy teaching in a nearby slum, and dialogical biblical exposition with Christian social workers in Latin America leave me convinced that the Bible is incredibly more true than most defenders of inerrancy ever realize.[137]

Pablo Richard

Pablo Richard, like many other Latin American liberation theologians, focuses on the theme of idolatry in his biblical exegesis.[138] In an engaging essay, "Biblical Theology of Confrontation with Idols," he traces the concept of idolatry in both Old and New Testaments, noting how the Bible both denies idolatry and affirms liberation.[139] In this affirmation of liberation there is the need for continuing struggle to free the oppressed from their idolatrous religious beliefs. Richard sees the book of Exodus in terms of violence: violence on the part of the Israelites against the violence of their Egyptian oppressors. Richard sees the inevitability of violence in the movement from idolatry to liberation as crucial for our times as it was for the world of the Bible.

Richard also takes pains to clarify the meaning of the phrase "people of God," a concept also used frequently by Míguez Bonino and José Comblin. Some thinkers have sought to identify the "people of God" with the popular church, distinguishing it from the formal, hierarchical church. But Richard prefers a more concrete, specific meaning, using the phrase to refer to the poor and oppressed who, because they have no power, are engaged in a constant uphill battle for justice and freedom. This is where the real church is to be found. Indeed, "to say 'church of the poor' is almost a redundancy; the church is either of the poor or it is not the church."[140] Richard by no means wishes to exclude the rich from the church, but he does believe that the rich should cease to be rich!

In identifying the people of God with the "church of the poor," Richard is critical of Rubem Alves and others who advocate a "theology of captivity." He believes that this view leads to a defeatist attitude that can only weaken the determination of the oppressed and harm their cause.

Juan Carlos Scannone

Juan Carlos Scannone has a special interest in the popular culture of Latin America.[141] His intent is to develop a "people's theology" that will show ordinary persons the real possibilities that are open to them as they strive for liberation.

Scannone uses the term "accompaniment"[142] to indicate that the role of theology is to accompany the oppressed in their quest for liberation, to read "the signs of God's presence in historical happenings,"[143] to criticize ideologies of both the left and the right in the light of God's word. The twofold task of theology is to analyze the de facto historical situation of oppression and then to reinterpret the Chirstian faith as a means for social transformation. Here the "theology of accompaniment" can help to open up new and unexpected opportunities for ordinary persons to achieve their liberation.

Adolfo Pérez Esquivel

Adolfo Pérez Esquivel is not a liberation theologian, but his sense of vocation exhibits what liberation theology is all about. The winner of the 1980 Nobel Peace Prize, Pérez Esquivel, an Argentinian, has spent much of his adult life traveling throughout Latin America advocating nonviolence through the organization he helped to establish, the Peace and Justice Service. His *Christ in a Poncho: Witnesses to the Nonviolent Struggles in Latin America* includes moving testimonials from various groups in Latin America speaking out for the rights of the poor.[144] "We are all the children of Medellín," says Pérez Esquivel.[145] He believes that the best hope for liberation in Latin America is neither capitalism nor communism, but a new form of socialization that would include something "on the order of self-management and sharing."[146]

Pérez Esquivel appreciates the contributions of Latin American liberation theologians, but he believes that insufficient attention has been devoted to a creative use of nonviolence. When he received his Nobel Peace Prize, he said:

> I want to receive this distinction in the name of the people of Latin America and, in a very special way, in the name of the poorest and smallest of my brothers and sisters because they are most beloved of God.[147]

In this preference for the poor as the "most beloved of God," Pérez Esquivel sums up the essence of Latin American liberation theology.[148]

THE PUEBLA CONFERENCE

The decade between the Medellín conference of 1968 (CELAM II) and the Puebla conference of 1979 (CELAM III) saw the proliferation of Latin American liberation theology. What began as a trickle in the late 1960s soon became a raging stream with many tributaries. If our discussion of more than a score of the prominent liberation theologians in Latin America has shown anything, it surely has indicated the plurality of their views and the richness of their thinking. Anyone who continues to caricature Latin American liberation theology as monolithic and kowtowing to a partyline of theological, social, and political thinking has done virtually no reading in this area.

But what impact have the Medellín conference and liberation theology had upon Latin America in the 1970s and early 1980s? The answer depends upon the answerer. Gustavo Gutiérrez suggested a positive view in 1982:

> The church is very different today. In 1968, there were buds of Christian communities committing themselves. Today there are masses. Today, personally, I am an optimist about liberation theology.[149]

But a Mexican bishop sees little change in what Medellín said and accomplished:

> Medellín is more a matter of what people say about it than of what really happened there. Read carefully, the commitments of Medellín do not oblige the church to side with the poor.[150]

Penny Lernoux, although claiming that the Medellín commitment to the poor was clear and irreversible, laments that "only a minority of bishops would heed its call."[151]

It is, of course, impossible to measure precisely the impact that Medellín and liberation theology had throughout Latin America during the 1970s. But two factors are obvious. First, principle enemies of liberation theology—poverty, hunger, oppression—became more pervasive. To quote the bishops of north-eastern Brazil in 1978: "If the Church were to summarize the past decade of 'development' in Latin America, it would have to state that the result is more hunger."[152]

And where there is more hunger, there is more oppression as those in power withhold food and the other necessities of life from those who have no power to acquire them on their own. Secondly, official opposition toward liberation theology from within the Catholic Church became more vocal.

A case in point is Archbishop Alfonso López Trujillo, who became the secretary general of CELAM in 1972. López Trujillo has been a leading spokesman of the conservative opposition within the church. His *Liberation or Revolution? An Examination of the Priest's Role in the Socio-Economic Class Struggle in Latin America* condemns liberation theology for shoring up Marxist revolution and reducing Christianity to radical politics.[153] The story of the struggle, and even intrigue, among church leaders in Latin America between Medellín and Puebla makes fascinating reading, but is too complex to relate here. One indication of the Vatican stance in this continuing controversy is the fact that in 1983 Pope John Paul II made López Trujillo a cardinal.

A preliminary document for the Puebla conference authored by López Trujillo and his staff appeared in 1977 and clearly reflected López Trujillo's conservative views. This document maintained that the social problems of Latin America must be solved gradually, doctrinal orthodoxy must be preserved at all costs, and the Medellín commitment to the poor should be deemphasized. Gustavo Gutiérrez was among the first to criticize this document for its total lack of social concern:

> I find that when we look at what it feels are the great problems that "touch the very heart of Christian civilization," poverty is not among them, nor are exploitation and social injustice, nor even the fact that these things are actually happening within countries "that call themselves Christian."[154]

Even the majority of Latin American bishops rejected this preliminary document as too weak and conservative. As a result, the document was revised and its conservative tone moderated.[155]

CELAM III was scheduled to be held in Puebla, Mexico, in the fall of 1978, but the sudden death of Pope John Paul I delayed the conference until early 1979. In his position as CELAM secretary general, López Trujillo was able to exert powerful influence in choosing official delegates and in designing the format of the conference. As a result, liberation theologians were virtually shut out of the official proceedings, although they did exert behind-the-scenes influence with their supportive bishops.

Pope John Paul II opened the conference and sought to steer a middle course between conservatives and liberals, condemning social injustice and oppression but objecting to close involvement in the political process on the part of priests. He pointed to Jesus as one who opposed all forms of injustice although not himself becoming a political activist. Jesus' mission, the pope declared, was to bring total salvation to all:

> [This task] imposes exacting demands on the attitude of any Christians who truly wish to serve the least of all their brothers and sisters, the poor, the needy, the marginalized.[156]

The Puebla documents cover a great many subjects, and both proponents and opponents of liberation theology can find sections that support their particular views. For example, capitalism is criticized for its "idolatrous worship of wealth in individualistic terms,"[157] and Marxism is condemned for its materialistic basis.[158] In opposing both systems, what the Puebla documents urge is:

> A new civilization that is just, fraternal, and open to the transcendent. It will also bear witness that eschatological hopes give vitality and meaning to human hopes.[159]

This statement, too, is subject to a variety of interpretations.

On a substantial, related matter, the Puebla conference was also important in that an unofficial women's group raised the issue of sexism, which had been ignored by Medellín and by most liberation theologians.

So what did the Puebla conference accomplish? It did not have the dramatic impact of its predecessor, Medellín. But beyond that commentators differ in their appraisal. Panamanian Bishop Marcus McGrath compares the two conferences:

> Medellín was a prophetic voice that didn't allow itself to be a mirror, reflecting on the reality of Latin America. Puebla, on the other hand, articulates the reality of Latin America but has not allowed itself to be a prophetic message.[160]

Gary MacEoin claims that the Puebla conference did not condemn liberation theology; it only ignored it.[161] Robert McAfee Brown points out that, considering the shenanigans that took place before and during the conference, "it is no small victory to be able to claim that it could have been a lot worse."[162]

Gustavo Gutiérrez applauds the positive gains of the conference:

> Puebla's viewpoint—the evangelizing potential of the poor—constitutes a definite advance over that of Medellín. Puebla has sought out a stance in creative continuity with its predecessor, and this position enables us to comprehend better the meaning of the liberating evangelization so much insisted upon, in recent years, by Medellín, by Puebla, and especially by the praxis of the Latin American church.[163]

Jon Sobrino adds that "the letter and spirit of the Medellín Conference is present in the Puebla Final Document."[164] And this is the crucial point. Medellín was convened during the passionate 1960s when the euphoria of Vatican II was still very much in evidence. The 1970s saw the growing strength of conservatism all over the world in the social, political, economic, and religious arenas. Because of this pervasive swing from liberalism to conservatism, there are grounds for surprise that the spirit of Medellín could survive as well as it did at Puebla a decade later. We can, therefore, agree with Michael Czerny's contention that the doors that opened at Medellín were not closed at Puebla; that, in fact, Puebla was "the Latin American Church's decision to employ Medellín for another ten years."[165]

VATICAN RESISTANCE

Latin American liberation theology remains a troubling phenomenon for Pope John Paul II and Vatican authorities. Cardinal Joseph Ratzinger, prefect of the Congregation for the Doctrine of the Faith, in early 1984 made allegations to Gutiérrez's ecclesiastical superiors in Peru that Gutiérrez had given a Marxist slant to his understanding of the Christian faith, and had sought to replace the hierarchical church with the people's church. These charges were considerably defused when the preeminent Catholic theologian Karl Rahner in March of 1984 wrote to Gutiérrez: "I have read all through your works and can find nothing in them that is against orthodoxy."[166] However, Brazilian priests Clodovis Boff and Antônio Moses and five other priests were removed from their teaching positions on pontifical faculties in 1984, and in September of that year Leonardo Boff ventured to Rome to defend his views. Six months later, the Vatican officially condemned some of his views concerning the hierarchical structure of the church.

In September of 1984, Ratzinger published a 35-page document entitled "Instruction on Certain Aspects of the Theology of Liberation." In some respects this document can be read as a vigorous defense of the basic affirmation of liberation theology:

> The scandal of the shocking inequality between the rich and the poor— whether between rich and poor countries, or between social classes in a single nation—is no longer tolerated. On the one hand, people have attained an unheard-of abundance which is given to waste, while on the other hand so many live in such poverty, deprived of the basic necessities, that one is hardly able even to count the victims of malnutrition.[167]

But the Ratzinger document also reechoes some of the common caricatures of Third World liberation theology—notably that this theology promotes liberation exclusively of an earthly and temporal kind; misuses the Bible to reduce liberation to political acts; restricts the meaning of sin to its social dimension at the expense of the personal; identifies the kingdom of God with human liberation movements; puts "one's trust in violent means in the hope of restoring more justice"; uses Marxist analysis without acknowledging a necessary connection between it and the basic Marxist ideology that includes "atheism and the denial of the human person, his liberty and his rights." It would be difficult to substantiate any one of these charges in the literature produced by Latin American liberation theologians. This may be why the document does not refer to even one theologian or text to verify any of its charges.

I shall return to these indictments of Third World liberation theology in the final chapter. Here I need only say, in summary, that one of the most eloquent affirmations of the central features of Latin American liberation theology was made in September 1984 in Canada:

> The needs of the poor must take priority over the desires of the rich, the rights of workers over the maximization of profits, the preservation of the environment over uncontrolled industrial expansion, production to meet social needs over production for military purposes. . . . The poor

people and poor nations . . . will judge those people who take these goods away from them, amassing to themselves the imperialistic monopoly of economic and political supremacy at the expense of others.[168]

The speaker was none other than Pope John Paul II.

CHAPTER THREE

African Liberation Theology

African liberation theology is not a mere clone of Latin American liberation theology. The diverse and rich culture of Africa, in addition to its unique experience of Christianity, represents a fresh challenge to those seeking to understand African notions of liberation.

As is well known, the Christian church has existed in northern Africa since early times. Especially prominent was the Christian community in Alexandria at the time of Clement and Origen in the second and third centuries. Later, in the fifth century, the Coptic Church of Egypt, which still flourishes today, emerged as an Egyptian nationalist movement opposing Byzantine imperialism. But it was not until the fifteenth century, with the arrival of Portuguese explorers, that Africa south of the Sahara came into contact with Western Christian imperialism. By the nineteenth century Christian missionaries were spreading throughout sub-Saharan Africa, usually joining forces with Western colonial powers in exploiting the inhabitants, their lands and resources, with a "prowhite, antiblack, we have the truth, you don't" attitude. As a result, racism and the aftertaste of slavery have deeply infected relationships between blacks and whites throughout Africa from the first colonial settlements to the present generation.

Thus, although stressing liberation from social, economic, and political oppression like its Latin American obverse, African liberation theology is deeply concerned with racial oppression. This component is especially strong in South Africa, where racism in the form of apartheid has been extremely virulent. Both African and North American black theologians have faulted Latin American theologians for failing to take the racial component seriously. As James Cone suggests:

The Latin American theologians' emphasis upon the class struggle, with almost no mention of race oppression, made black theologians suspicious of their white European identity.[1]

Ruvimbo Tekere of Zimbabwe also notes:

> The fact that the cultures of the Indians and blacks have been ignored
> seems to indicate why they are absent from the larger participation in
> Latin American life. . . . The rich cultural attributes of the Indians and
> the blacks have been ignored by the church in conformity with the ruling
> dominant class.[2]

But in countries other than South Africa the racial component is not so
important. John Pobee points out:

> With the exception of the Republic of South Africa, racial prejudice is
> not so bad in Africa as in America. . . . Consequently, African theology,
> though interested in liberation, is not preoccupied with liberation as
> much as black theology is.[3]

In addition, African theologians have in recent years had a far greater
appreciation for indigenous religions than have their Latin American counterparts. Even the African Christian churches have begun to show a willingness to
incorporate indigenous beliefs and practices into their teachings. This, however, has not always been the case. The early missionaries who came from the
First World brought with them a westernized version of Christianity that
looked upon the African blacks as heathen and Africa itself as the "empire of
Satan." These missionaries were convinced that either the Africans had no
religion at all or what religion they had was pagan. In fact, perhaps the most
potent factor in the development of independent churches throughout Africa
was the failure of mission programs of the established churches to come to
terms with the African religious heritage.

Even today the "indigenization" issue has not failed to generate controversy.
On the one hand, the Christian churches would have difficulty coming to terms
with certain African customs—for example, polygamy. On the other hand,
some theologians, especially in South Africa, have complained that the return
to African roots has amounted to a digression from the burning social, racial,
and economic issues of the day. Unlike most of their Latin American counterparts, African theologians have been more sharply divided between those who
favor indigenization as a way of retrieving their African heritage, and those
who favor indigenization as a way of liberating the oppressed. Indeed, the
latter group would not consider the former group to be liberation theologians
in the true sense of the term. It is surprising to discover that many African
theologians, for whom indigenization is so important in liberating African
religion from foreign intrusion, are less involved than most South African
theologians in the social problems that impede human liberation. Gwinyai
Muzorewa muses:

> It is not clear why most Africans tend to shy away from politicizing their
> theology. In my opinion, both theologies are concerned about restoring

the proper image of black humanity, an image which had been grossly distorted by Europeans and white Americans.[4]

Here we shall not attempt to make a distinction between African theology and African black theology.[5] It is far better to think of these terms, as Muzorewa suggests, as expressions of two different emphases which are important within an all-encompassing theology of liberation.[6] If we can be critical of some forms of African theology—especially outside South Africa—for stressing indigenization at the expense of involvement in social issues, we can be equally critical of most forms of Latin American liberation theology for stressing social issues at the expense of indigenization. Here Ruvimbo Tekere of Zimbabwe is on target in his criticism of Latin American liberation theology:

A marriage of these cultures, traditional and Christian, is critical for Latin American liberation theology. Traditional or native culture is not opposed to the gospel. Only in such a marriage, when the oppressed and dominated feel they have a heritage that contributes positively to the present will they participate fully in the Christian church without a schizophrenic identity of "Christian" and "heathen."[7]

I shall have occasion to refer to the indigenization issue throughout this chapter.

So where can we begin our discussion of African liberation theology? In a book of this size I shall confine the discussion primarily, but not exclusively, to South Africa, where liberation theology has been particularly strong in its concern for social issues. A brief historical sketch of Christianity prior to the emergence of black theology in the 1960s seems in order.

SOUTH AFRICA: A PORTRAIT OF OPPRESSION

White settlers from Holland landed in South Africa in 1652 and established a sailing settlement near what is now the city of Cape Town. In a manner reminiscent of the white invaders of North America, who pushed the Amerindians westward, the Dutch settlers forced the native blacks into the midsection of Africa. White immigrants, the progenitors of the contemporary Afrikaners, came in increasing numbers from many European countries and combined their forces against the native blacks. British citizens began to settle during the latter part of the eighteenth century and for a time served as a buffer between the Afrikaners and the indigenous black population. The British, however, greedy for gold, moved to the interior, an invasion that led to the Anglo-Boer Wars (1899–1901). The victorious British soon united all of South Africa into one white-controlled principality in which blacks had no rights—a wholesale oppression that was continued when England gave commonwealth status to the Union of South Africa in 1910. The Afrikaners began to establish their own identity by emphasizing their own culture, tradition, and language. Their Nationalist Party, founded in 1914, made a concerted effort to institutionalize apartheid in a ruthless enactment of laws to keep blacks powerless. The Nationalist Party, which has held power since 1948, reaffirmed apartheid in the constitutional referendum of November 1983, allowing partial parliamentary recognition for Asians and "coloureds," but keeping the blacks powerless.

In this resolute affirmation of white supremacy, most Afrikaners believed they were building a Christian nation and, until recently, were supported by their "Christian" (that is, *white*) churches. The Dutch Reformed Church continues to be the largest and most influential church, often referred to as "the Nationalist Party at prayer." Ernie Regehr points out the importance of this church and its relationship to the government:

> It is a potent irony that one of today's most perverted and unjust social systems is the creation of a regime that, perhaps more than any other modern state, views itself as a Christian theocracy. Since 1948, when the Afrikaner nationalists gained power, the Dutch Reformed churches have had direct access to, if not control over, the country's political leadership.[8]

Similar to what happened in Latin America, the system of apartheid—oppressor versus oppressed—was not only condoned by the white parent churches of the First World, which gave financial support to their mission churches in Africa, but was also reinforced by First World investors from western Europe and the United States, primarily through transnational corporations. The participation of U.S. businesses in the economic system of South Africa has increased in recent decades. In the words of Baldwin Sjollema:

> Those who invest in South Africa should please do so with their eyes open. . . . Economic growth [has] failed to benefit black people in any significant way. The claim by transnational corporations that the apartheid system would change and human rights improve has also not come true.[9]

There is little doubt that a direct correlation exists between economic and political domination by First World powers and the perpetuation of apartheid in South Africa.

THE EMERGENCE OF BLACK CONSCIOUSNESS

Through the years blacks have tried to retaliate, but with little success. As early as 1912 they established the Native National Congress, which later became the African National Congress. In the early 1960s South Africa withdrew from the British Commonwealth and became a republic. This was an especially important period in the emergence of black consciousness. The

Sharpeville massacre (1960), in which seventy blacks who engaged in a peaceful demonstration were slaughtered, led to protests, boycotts, and strikes, which served to stiffen black resistance. The African National Congress, for many years under the dynamic leadership of Nobel Peace Prize winner Albert Luthuli, took an increasingly active role while maintaining its nonviolent stance.

The multiracial University Christian Movement (UCM), established in 1967, attracted large numbers of black students because of its willingness to take stands on social and political issues. But many black students withdrew from it in 1969 to form the all-black South African Students Organization (SASO), motivated in large part by the inspiring leadership of the late Steve Biko.

Another important organization that cultivated black consciousness was the Christian Institute, founded in 1963 by C. F. Beyers Naudé. The Christian Institute later became a part of the South African Council of Churches, which in 1968 published "A Message to the People of South Africa" condemning apartheid. As a result of its aggressive pro-black policy, the Christian Institute became a target of government espionage and was forced to close in 1977. It had been a major force in encouraging black consciousness in the 1960s and 1970s:

> On a theological level, the Institute had an impact in southern Africa similar to that of liberation theology in Latin America, which challenges Christians to accept the scriptural injunction to work and *be* with the poor. . . . The real threat posed by the Christian Institute lay not in its calls for some reforms, but in its call for truly radical change—at the roots of society.[10]

By the early 1970s black theology had begun to make an appearance in South Africa—at the same time that Latin American liberation theology was emerging. One of the first books on this subject was *Black Theology: The South African Voice*, edited by Basil Moore.[11] Both the book and its editor, the former secretary general of the University Christian Movement in South Africa, were banned. In his introductory article, "What is Black Theology?," Moore points out that the term "black theology" originated in the United States in the late 1960s. He goes on to stress that it is imperative for South African theologians to apply this new theology to their own historical situation:

> [Black theology] starts with black people in the South African situation facing the strangling problems of oppression, fear, hunger, insult and dehumanization. It tries to understand as clearly as possible who these people are, what their life experiences are, and the nature and cause of their suffering. This is an indispensable datum of Black theology.[12]

Moore points to the concept of "Christ is black" as an important one, indicating God's identification with an oppressed people.

In South Africa there has been a vigorous effort on the part of black liberation theologians to relate their understanding of the Christian gospel to apartheid and the various social evils imbedded in this racist society. Four of these theologians merit special consideration.

Steve Biko

Steve Biko is one of the many courageous blacks in South Africa who have given their lives for their convictions. I have already noted how he was instrumental in founding SASO in 1969, whose manifesto on black consciousness merits quoting:

> 1. The basic tenet of Black Consciousness is that the black man must reject all value systems that seek to make him a foreigner in the country of his birth and reduce his basic human dignity;
> 2. The black man must build up his own value system, and see himself as self-defined and not as defined by others;
> 3. The concept of Black Consciousness implies the awareness by the black people of the power they wield as a group, both economically and politically, and hence group cohesion and solidarity are important facets of Black Consciousness;
> 4. Black Consciousness will always be enhanced by the totality of involvement of the oppressed people, hence the message of Black Consciousness has to be spread to reach all sections of the black community.[13]

By the early 1970s Biko had become a forceful advocate of black consciousness and black theology, contending that the role of black theology is to give South Africa "a more human face." In 1972 he wrote a biting article in defense of black consciousness, affirming that:

> We are aware that the white man is sitting at our table. We know that he has no right to be there; we want to remove him from our table, strip the table of all the trappings put on it by him, decorate it in true African style, settle down and then ask him to join us on our terms if he wishes.[14]

Biko consistently and steadfastly argued that the basic problem in South Africa is not class struggle, but racism. Here, as already noted, is an important difference between South African and Latin American liberation theology. One might argue that the historical situations are radically different, but even so Latin American liberation theologians can be faulted for their neglect of the racial component. Alfred Reid of Jamaica asks:

> Where is the contribution of the 40 million blacks of Brazil? What mark have they made on the life and thought of the Christian community?

What about the blacks of Nicaragua? What fellowship is there with the Caribbean, with Guyana and Belize, which are part of this continent?[15]

The reason for stressing the racial component is the conviction that whites really do believe that blacks are inferior. The problem with racial integration, as Biko saw it, is that white values would continue to dominate. What blacks must do is emphasize group pride. In order to accomplish this, they must define their worth in their own terms. Biko believed that a new appreciation of the Christian gospel will find God and Christ siding with the racially oppressed.

During the 1970s Biko was in and out of jail and often under house arrest. Efforts on the part of government authorities to silence him only heightened his efforts in support of black consciousness throughout South Africa. Finally, on September 6, 1977, Biko was arrested and taken to jail at Port Elizabeth, Cape Province, where he was tortured. He died six days later. At Biko's funeral Bishop Desmond Tutu spoke these words:

God called Steve Biko to be his servant in South Africa—to speak on behalf of God. . . . God called him to be the founder of the Black Consciousness Movement. . . . Steve has started something that is quite unstoppable. The powers of evil, of injustice, of oppression, of exploitation, have done their worst and they have lost. They have lost because they are immoral and wrong, and our God, the God of Exodus, the liberator God, is a God of justice and liberation and goodness.[16]

One of Biko's most ardent supporters was the white newspaperman Donald Woods, who later escaped from South Africa when he was under house arrest. Woods wrote of Biko:

If the nationalists had allowed Steve Biko to operate unfettered, within the bounds of normal law, apartheid could have been negotiated out of existence within five years for the benefit of all South Africans of every race.[17]

But because this was not to be, Woods continued, "the express train of white racism is now rushing at full speed on a collision course with the express train of black anger."[18]

Bishop Desmond Tutu

Bishop Desmond Tutu is another vigorous advocate of black consciousness who remains "on the front lines."[19] Tutu has served since 1978 as secretary general of the South African Council of Churches, and in 1984 was the first black to be elected the Anglican bishop of Johannesburg. He has never hesitated to speak out on racial issues, both at home and abroad. In 1980 his passport was confiscated after he told an audience in Denmark that that country should boycott South African coal. In 1981 he was permitted to go to Europe and once again he lost his passport, this time for declaring the South African regime the most savage since that of Nazi Germany. But Desmond Tutu is not to be silenced. In 1984, he was awarded the Nobel Peace Prize for his vigorous defense of human rights.

A champion of human dignity, Tutu is also a strong proponent of a South African black theology:

> We have in our midst now the Theology of Liberation, as developed in Latin America, and Black Theology developed in the USA and Southern Africa. The perplexity they have to deal with is this: why does suffering single out black people so conspicuously, suffering not at the hands of pagans or other unbelievers, but at the hands of white fellow Christians who claim allegiance to the same Lord and Master?[20]

Speaking to white students at Witwatersrand University in 1980, Tutu issued this challenge:

> We are committed to black liberation because thereby we are committed to white liberation. You will never be free until we blacks are free. So join the liberation struggle.[21]

About the same time he stated, "I want to declare categorically that I believe apartheid to be evil and immoral and therefore unchristian."[22]

Tutu predicts that there will be a black prime minister in South Africa by 1990.

Allan Boesak

Another prominent black theologian in South Africa is Allan Boesak.[23] Chaplain at the University of the Western Cape and president of the World Alliance of Reformed Churches, Boesak's most important book to date is *Farewell to Innocence: A Socio-Ethical Study on Black Theology and Power.*[24] In it he points out the difficulty of expounding liberation theology in the midst of the acute political crisis in South Africa. He defines black theology as:

> The theological reflection of black Christians on the situation in which they live and on their struggle for liberation.[25]

He goes on to ask:

> What does it mean to believe in Jesus Christ when one is black and living in a world controlled by white racists? And what if these racists call themselves Christians also?[26]

Boesak believes that this is a time of a "farewell to innocence" for whites, including those white liberals who like to "do things" for blacks. In language reminiscent of many Latin American liberation theologians, Boesak views Yahweh as the liberator God, and Jesus as the one who affirms liberation for the oppressed. "To confess Jesus Christ as the Black Messiah is the only true confession of our time."[27]

Like other black South African theologians, Boesak differs from Latin American theologians in stressing the sin of racism. But by no means does he consider racism the only issue:

> While absolutely not minimizing racism as a demonic, pseudo-religious ideology (who, coming from South Africa, can?) we must nevertheless ask: Is racism indeed the only issue? It seems to us that there is a far deeper malady in the American and South African societies that manifests itself in the form of racism. . . . Black theologians still fail to see what was seen by Martin Luther King and Malcolm X: The relation between racism and capitalism. . . . Black Theology, then, must mean a search for a totally new social order, and in this search it will have to drink deep from the well of African tradition.[28]

Boesak takes pains to point out that the Christian gospel transcends all ideologies and national aspirations. To have political preferences, he says, is not wrong; but it is wrong to equate these preferences with the Christian gospel. Boesak rejects the approach to black theology that makes black *the* symbol of oppression, for this only serves to absolutize one's own particular racial ideology. Although pointing out the errors of capitalism, he does not extol the virtues of socialism. Rather, he opts for a social democracy in which all citizens would have the opportunity to take part in the decisions that affect their lives.

Boesak also believes it important that liberation theologians from all over the world work together despite their different historical situations:

> While we acknowledge that all expressions of liberation theology are not identical, we must protest very strongly against the total division (and contrast) some make between Black Theology in South Africa and Black Theology in the United States; between Black Theology and African Theology; between Black Theology and the Latin American theology of liberation. As a matter of principle, we have therefore treated all these different expressions within the framework where they belong: the framework of the theology of liberation.[29]

It is important to underscore Boesak's insistence that African theology and black theology should not be separated.

Another important feature of Allan Boesak's own theological perspective is his contention that liberation theology is a direct descendent of the Reformed tradition associated with John Calvin. Boesak's *Black and Reformed: Apartheid, Liberation, and the Calvinist Tradition* documents this strong historical continuity.[30] He quotes extensively from the writings of John Calvin to show that apartheid is completely alien to the Reformed tradition, and concludes:

> It is my conviction that the reformed tradition has a future in this country only if black Reformed Christians are willing to take it up, make it truly their own, and let this tradition once again become what it once was: a champion of the cause of the poor and the oppressed, clinging to the confession of the lordship of Christ and to the supremacy of the word of God.[31]

Among Boesak's greatest strengths are his willingness to build bridges of cooperation with liberation theologians of every type and his desire to uncover the rich resources of his own religious tradition.

Manas Buthelezi

Another important South African theologian is Manas Buthelezi. He is a good example of those African liberation theologians who disavow African tradition and culture as the cornerstone of African liberation theology. For Buthelezi, theology must first be grounded in the present-day sufferings of the oppressed. He distinguishes two approaches to the development of an indigenous theology in South Africa: the ethnographic and the anthropological. By the former he means the attempt to uncover African worldviews and myths that will serve as the conceptual frame of reference for African theology. He objects to this approach, which he contends overlooks present-day realities and seeks a historical overview blind to immediate social issues. He opts for the anthropological methodology that begins with the contemporary situation, focusing on factors that reveal the continuing oppression and dehumanization of blacks. In contrasting these two approaches, he writes:

> Pride in one's traditional heritage is the fruit of pride in one's dignity as a man. A self-despising man is ashamed of his past as well as of anything that is related to him. Any proposal that this man should go back to his traditional customs will only serve to enslave his mind more, since he is not yet psychologically redeemed. I am suspicious of "African experts" who, without being invited, come from outside our black experience and propose theological as well as sociological programmes showing how the past cultural patterns can shape and condition our lives today. It must be a black man who knows how best to live as a black man today. A relevant message of the Gospel is that which not only helps the black man to regain his self-confidence and respect as a human being, but which focuses attention on the removal of the dehumanizing facets of modern life.[32]

Buthelezi insists, then, that an overemphasis on African traditional religions can numb blacks to the serious, contemporary social issues they face. Theology must above all else reflect "the throbbings of the life situation in which people find themselves."[33] Black theology in South Africa must begin in "Johannesburg, Durban and Cape Town"; not in the resuscitation of an "old traditional world."[34] Buthelezi suggests a "theology of restlessness," which keeps blacks on their toes, alert to the essential social changes that must take place if they are to achieve their liberation.

South African black liberation theologians are united in making liberation from all forms of human oppression their focal point. Without minimizing the economic and political dimensions of oppression, they see racism as the number one enemy of blacks. But at the same time they warn against making black theology primarily a tool of black power and black nationalism. For this reason they want to make contact with liberation theologians throughout the Third World, for whom oppression takes on different features. On the issue of indigenization some of them—Desmond Tutu, for example—see positive values in it, whereas others—Manas Buthelezi, for example—although not unilaterally opposing it, worry that such a concern may divert attention from burning contemporary social issues.

THE SEARCH FOR INDIGENOUS AFRICAN RELIGIONS

It is important that we give some attention to African theologians outside South Africa. In doing so we shall see that their dominant concern is not so much basic contemporary social and political issues as it is the search for an indigenous African religion. One of the real problems in uncovering the native African religions has been the dearth of written accounts and the dependence on oral tradition. There is general agreement that a written African theology has largely been a by-product of the introduction of the Bible by Western missionaries. As late as the mid-1960s, Bolaji Idowu of Nigeria had chastized African theologians for their failure to relate Christianity to its African context, a charge later reinforced by John Mbiti of Kenya, who has said that "the Church in Africa is a Church without a theology and a Church without theological concern."[35] Bengt Sundkler had earlier pleaded for an interpretation of Christianity that would be indigenous to the African situation:

> Theology in Africa has to interpret . . . Christ in terms that are relevant and essential to African existence. . . . A theologian who with the apostle Paul is prepared to become . . . unto Africans as African must start with the fundamental facts of the African interpretation of existence and the universe.[36]

Similarly, Harry Sawyerr maintained:

> Once it is realized that it is not necessary for the African to become detribalized to become a Christian, the Christianization of pagan cus-

toms and beliefs would seem to be the most natural and reasonable means of re-establishing culture.[37]

Aylward Shorter

Aylward Shorter of Uganda has had as his primary concern finding parallels between Christianity and native African religions. An anthropologist by training, Shorter's major work is *African Christian Theology: Adaptation or Incarnation?*[38] He notes the extreme complexity to be found in African traditional religion and points out that a thorough survey of the subject would mean "853 tribes to be studied in the African continent. We should obviously have to wait a long time for the needed 853 African scholars of religion to make their appearance."[39] Despite this tremendous diversity, several common themes, Shorter notes, recur in African religion: a close relationship between the living and the dead; the search for the abundant life; the importance of community.

In his writings Shorter expresses convictions at the heart of liberation theology—namely, the importance of contextualization and the need to develop theology "from below." Shorter believes that the symbol of Christ as black is useful in placing Christ on the side of the poor and oppressed. Shorter's special contribution has been to combine his anthropological interest in African religious traditions with his own profound concern for human liberation.

John Mbiti

Another important figure in the development of an indigenous African theology is John Mbiti of Kenya. Formerly director of the Ecumenical Institute in Bossey, Switzerland, Mbiti has been a pioneer in uncovering the roots of traditional African religion. He insists that Christian missionaries did not introduce Africans to the true God. On the contrary, God through the centuries has been as active among African peoples as among the Jewish people. His pioneering book, *Concepts of God in Africa* (1970), examines three hundred African peoples with regard to indigenization.[40] His subsequent research has confirmed the importance of indigenization, indicating that African Christian leaders, rather than receiving their "theological circumcision" in the First World, should begin with their own religious heritage. Mbiti even suggests that "as the axis of Christianity tilts southward," the World Council of Churches should consider moving its headquarters from Geneva to Kinshasa, and that the Catholic Church should ponder moving the Vatican from Rome to Kampala.[41]

Mbiti criticizes some forms of African liberation theology for lacking an adequate biblical basis:

This neglect in Africa of the biblical backing of the theology of liberation is a very alarming omission that calls currently for correction; otherwise that branch of African theology will lose its credibility.[42]

He also rebukes those who ally themselves too closely with some extreme forms of American black theology. Mbiti sees American black theology as an import having little relevance to the African situation. He condemns American black theology for its undue emphasis on the theme of liberation, its divisiveness in using the term "black" in reference to God and Christ, and its stress on the negative dimension of oppression instead of on the positive dimension of joy:

> African theology has no interest in coloring God or Christ black, no interest in reading liberation into every text, no interest in telling people to think or act "black."[43]

Mbiti's attack on American black theology has met with a mixed response from his colleagues. On the one hand, Desmond Tutu believes that Mbiti's attacks on black theology are unwarranted: for Tutu, African theology, African black theology, and American black theology must be allies, not antagonists. On the other hand, Allan Boesak has been critical of black theologians who make black *the* symbol of oppression and he singles out American theologian James Cone as particularly vulnerable to this charge.[44]

Mbiti has been a thorn in the flesh for the more radical African and American black theologians. But surely this does not make Mbiti any less a theologian of liberation, unless this term is defined in a very narrow sense. He is an African theologian who has shown a continuing interest in relating Christianity to the indigenous African setting—"There is a Christian Yes to African religiosity"[45]—yet a theologian who believes that Christian theology must transcend contemporary social issues and ideologies. At this point he is closer to Allan Boesak than some of his critics care to admit.

E. W. Fashole-Luke

Another theologian interested in the recovery of an indigenous African theology is E. W. Fashole-Luke of Sierra Leone. Fashole-Luke believes it important for African Christianity "to suit the tongue, style, genius, character and culture of African peoples."[46] He faults John Mbiti for not explaining sufficiently the proper relationship between the Christian faith, the lesser African deities, and ancestor worship. Yet, with Mbiti, he also believes it important for African theology to transcend cultural, racial, and ethical categories in its espousal of a theology of liberation for both oppressor and oppressed.

Kwesi Dickson

Kwesi Dickson of Ghana also stresses the importance of developing an indigenous African theology. The early missionaries who came from the First World held the misplaced notion that their brand of Christianity would soon make the native religions obsolete. But the truth is quite the contrary. In fact,

Dickson believes that native beliefs are so strong and pervasive that on critical life issues most African Christians would not hesitate to shed their Christian beliefs and practices, and return to their native customs. For this reason, Dickson believes it incumbent upon African Christians to incorporate native elements into their churches. He suggests a "theology of selfhood," by which he means an affirmation of African humanity and ethos—a theology that would transcend the various particularities of religion and culture, and focus on those basic qualities shared by all Africans.[47]

Charles Nyamiti

Charles Nyamiti of Tanzania makes an important contribution when he distinguishes three contemporary approaches to African theology: the speculative model, which relies on Western categories of thinking; the socio-biblical approach, which focuses on the biblical proclamation; and the militant model, which has liberation as its main theme. Nyamiti believes that all three approaches must continue to have their place in African theology and that all of them should have as their overriding purpose a creative combination of Christianity and African values. Like John Mbiti, Nyamiti criticizes African black theology for its overemphasis on liberation, warning that African theology is too vast and complex to be reduced to one theme.

Lamin Sanneh

Lamin Sanneh, formerly on the faculty at the University of Ibadan and then at Harvard University, is especially important for his scholarly studies of the religious traditions of the countries of West Africa. In his *West African Christianity: The Religious Impact,* Sanneh stresses the importance of a proper appreciation of indigenous African religions, pointing out the irony

> that missionary Christianity as the propounder of a universal God turned out to be an exclusive religion tied to an ethnocentric Western world view, whereas traditional religions, criticized as restrictive tribal affairs, offered hope and reconciliation by their tolerance of religious diversity and by their inclusive view of human community. This makes them more in tune with Biblical teaching than the politically divisive form of European Christianity.[48]

Kofi Appiah-Kubi

Kofi Appiah-Kubi of Ghana believes that the main reason for the rise of independent churches—he prefers to call them indigenous churches—has been the failure on the part of the established missionary churches to satiate African spiritual hunger. Indeed, he considers this spiritual factor more critical even than the failure of the established churches to deal with social issues. He also faults the established churches for their neglect of the gift of healing, so central to the indigenous churches and their insistence that worship and healing go hand in hand.

Appiah-Kubi is a leader in encouraging African Christians to develop their own liturgies and belief-systems, and he wants Africans to have nothing more to do with Western, white traditions. He stresses, for example, the need for a close and vital connection between the Holy Spirit and the deeply imbedded African custom of ancestor worship. A reverence for the spirits of the dead is not unlike a belief in the Holy Spirit.

Mercy Amba Oduyọye

Mercy Amba Oduyọye of Nigeria elaborates on what she calls "beings-in-relation," by which she means the communal dimension of African life—a theme common to many African theologians.[49] For Oduyọye, there can be no separation between the sacred and the secular, body and spirit, male and female, past and present. For the African, the individual is secondary, the community is primary. Christianity needs to find African ways to express convictions that emphasize the common spiritual bond among all peoples and all things. For example, African belief in the existence of spirits, of the close, continuing relationship between the living and the dead, and even of witch-craft, are manifestations of the spiritual continuum so vital to both Christianity and African religion.

Oduyọye is also a pioneer in challenging Third World theologians to put at the top of their agenda the concerns of women. They must be accepted as full-fledged members of a truly liberated human community. She sharply criticizes many of her male colleagues for failing to appreciate that sexism is "part of the intricate web of oppression in which most of us live." She urges that "women's experience should become a part of the 'community of interpretation' not only of Scripture but of the whole Christian tradition."[50]

Engelbert Mveng

Engelbert Mveng of Cameroun has noted some sharp rifts opening up between African and Latin American liberation theologians. He points out, for example, that the Ecumenical Association of Third World Theologians (EATWOT) was neither Latin American nor Asian in its origins, but African. EATWOT, therefore, is not simply "an institutionalization of the Latin American theology of liberation." He criticizes EATWOT for neither taking Africa seriously nor taking into account the minority groups to be found in Latin America:

Who has the right to speak in the Third World? Why are there so many absent, so many forgotten? Is it too early to invite the Australian aborigenes? The blacks of Brazil, and the native Latin Americans—all the descendents of the Incas, the Aztecs, and all those basic Christian communities that dot the rainforests, the mountain ranges, and the pampas—where are *their* representatives? What about *their* way of encountering Christ or turning from him, of *their* way of building, and living, church, of being the people of God—who will tell us of all this if they are absent? How shall we fashion a theology of the Third World without them? What kind of "Third World Theology" would we have if it were a theology they would not recognize?[51]

Mveng's warning is well taken. If liberation theologians truly believe that theology begins with "the underside of history" in terms of their particular situations, then they must expect that theology will vary according to each historical context. They must beware of an elitism that makes certain features of liberation theology normative for everyone else. They must be sensitive to minority groups in their own backyard—groups that may have slipped through their liberation net.

CHRISTIAN FAITHS AND AFRICAN BELIEFS

The relationship between the Christian faith and African beliefs and practices remains a troubling issue for many of the Christian churches, particularly when such beliefs and practices go against the grain of normative Western teachings. What about the deeply imbedded African custom of polygamy, for example? Does authentic human liberation mean freedom *from* or freedom *for* the practice of polygamy? Two authors consider this issue sympathetically.

In his *Polygamy Reconsidered: African Plural Marriage and the Christian Churches,* Eugene Hillman, a Catholic priest who lived many years with the Masei people of Tanzania, warns the church against issuing moral directives from the perspective of foreign—Western—culture. He argues that Western Christians need to have a deeper appreciation of the values that polygamy has served in African society:

> Not only does this custom serve as a dynamic principle of family survival, growth, security, continuity, and prestige, but it has, also, an integrating function within the kinship system. There are a number of fairly obvious ways through which polygamy can contribute to the solidarity and prosperity of groups on different levels of society.[52]

In his *African Widows,* Michael Kirwen, a Catholic priest who has spent considerable time with the Luo people in Tanzania, affirms the value of the leviratic custom in which a widow cohabitates with her brother-in-law, who becomes a substitute for her deceased husband. He argues:

> The leviratic custom is compatible with Christian doctrine on marriage, no matter how frequently it occurs; it promotes Christian marital values

and is an acceptable relationship within and by members of Christian communities.[53]

Surely any developed theology of liberation must come to terms with the "polygamy problem" in the same way that it confronts other critical social issues.

The confrontation between imported Western theology and indigenous African theology came to a crisis in the mid-1970s, although, to be sure, it had been festering for many years. At the third assembly of the All African Conference of Churches meeting in Zambia in 1974, the delegates officially adopted and recommended to their churches what was called a moratorium policy. This policy urged that for a period of five years the First World stop sending money and missionary personnel to the Third World, a proposal that arose less from hostility and more from the desire to assume responsibility for one's own destiny, one of the goals of liberation theology.

This resolution, under the guidance of John Gatu, then secretary general of the Presbyterian Church in East Africa, and Burgess Carr, who teaches at Yale Divinity School, was a clear indication of the failure of traditional Western-oriented missionary programs and the need for African churches to develop their own leadership and resources. Although the moratorium policy was never fully put into practice, it did reveal the restless independent African spirit and led to a gradual yet significant change in the relationship between the older Western and younger African churches.[54]

As we have seen, Latin American liberation theology can no more be exported to Africa than it can be imported to North America. Emphases will be different and will reflect varying stages of growth in the development of a full-blown, all embracing liberation theology. If many African theologians can be faulted for lack of sufficient attention to certain basic social, political, and economic issues, many Latin American theologians can be criticized for neglecting autochthonous religions. African theology will inevitably take on its own forms as Africans take their destiny into their own hands. What Eugene Hillman says of the proper response of the church to the African practice of polygamy applies equally well to the proper attitude toward the emerging varieties of African liberation theology:

To learn from others: this is a call to transcend our cultural limitations and congenital blindness. To do this, even partially, is to achieve a measure of liberation, a new vantage point, a broader horizon, a fresh vision of the world, a better look at humanity and what it means to be human.[55]

CHAPTER FOUR

Asian Liberation Theology

The vast, sprawling continent of Asia exhibits even more variety than do Africa and Latin America. Each country has its own distinctive history and traditions, and each has had its own unique encounter with Western colonialism. More than 85 percent of all Asians suffer from abject poverty and oppression.

An added ingredient in the Asian setting is the living presence of many major religions competing for the allegiance of humankind. To be sure, Latin America has its indigenous religions—heretofore largely ignored by their liberation theologians—but Catholicism has been the dominant faith there for the past four centuries. Native African religions have not only survived the aggression of Christian and Muslim invaders, but have become a rich source of spiritual insights for African theologians. The situation in Asia is unique, however, for here we find Hinduism, Buddhism, Confucianism, and other religious traditions coexisting in an infinite variety, compounding rather than alleviating certain forms of human oppression—for example, discrimination against women. A further complicating factor is that Asian Christians are a tiny minority, with but 3 percent of Asians identifying themselves as Christians and with only the Philippines claiming a majority of Christians. It is ironic that most contemporary Asians consider Christianity, despite its roots in the Middle East, a foreign religion, a product of Western colonial expansion![1]

Asian liberation theology has thus had to contend with two additional components that set it apart from most forms of liberation theology in Latin America and Africa. First, it daily encounters other major living religions. Secondly, in most Asian countries Christianity is a very small minority group. Both of these factors have had a profound impact on the content and methods of liberation theology in that part of the world.

Christianity—Protestantism in particular—had very little impact in Asia until the nineteenth century, which witnessed the rapid growth of First World missionary societies that established outposts throughout the continent. Like their Latin American and African counterparts, most Western missionaries stressed the importance of individual conversion to Christ, with little emphasis on the social dimension and with even less appreciation for the positive values to be found in other religions. In the twentieth century the burgeoning of anticolonial, anti-Western sentiment has seen the development of forms of Christianity divested of foreign cultural baggage and leadership, a step vitally necessary to the survival of Christianity in Asia. U Ba Hmyn of Burma set the future course clearly at the third assembly of the World Council of Churches in New Delhi in 1961 when he said:

> No theology will deserve to be called ecumenical in the coming days which ignores Asian structures. It may use the term "ecumenical," but it will really be parochial and Western only.[2]

There is no adequate way to give even a postcard summary of developments in recent Asian theology that have led to the emergence of liberation theology. My strategy will be to select a few countries and a few theologians who are forging theologies unique to their own particular situation. It must be borne in mind, however, that these are but "samplings" of the many creative religious thinkers who would be unanimous in warning us that Asia is a many-splendored continent; it demands many distinctive strategies tailored to the indigenous specifications of particular areas.

JAPAN

Although Japan is not a Third World country, its influence throughout Asia is too great to be ignored here. Ever since the Catholic missionary Francis Xavier set foot in Japan in 1549, to be followed by Protestant missionaries only in 1859, Christianity and Japan have entertained a love-hate relationship. At the outset, Catholicism spread with amazing rapidity, owing in large part to the desire of the Japanese to engage in trade with the West. But by 1636 the proliferation of this "foreign religion" had become a threat to Japan and its own deeply imbedded traditions. That year the Japanese government promulgated the Closed Country Edict, which kept foreigners out of the country for the next two centuries. With the arrival of Commodore Perry in the mid-1850s, the gates were forced open and Protestant missionaries were among the first to enter. Much later, concerned about the proliferation of Protestant denominations, the Japanese government finally forced many of their churches to merge into one body, the Kyodon, a union that began to break up after the Second World War.

Probably no other Asian Christian made such a large impact outside Asia in the twentieth century than Toyohiko Kagawa. A world traveler and prolific author, Kagawa played an influential role, not only as a Christian ecumenist, pacifist, and poet, but as a social reformer who insisted that true Christianity must be practiced "at the counter, in the kitchen, or in the shop."[3]

European theology had been so strong in Japan that only in the 1960s younger theologians began to cry: "Deliver Japanese theology from German captivity!"[4] The 1960s witnessed growing resistance to neocolonialism, combined with an upsurge of secularism and religious pluralism, all of which had a powerful impact upon Christian Japanese theologians as they sought to articulate a theological stance more in tune with their Asian setting. Kazoh Kitamori, the late professor of systematic theology at Tokyo Union Theological Seminary, anticipated this development in his groundbreaking book *Theology of the Pain of God* (1965). In a manner reminiscent of Dietrich Bonhoeffer and some Latin American liberation theologians, Kitamori argued that pain is a part of God's nature and that the recovery of this dimension of God as related to human oppression is the most important task for Japanese theology.

Kosuke Koyama

The leading liberation theologian with Japanese roots is Kosuke Koyama. His influence extends far beyond the land of his birth. Koyama has spent most of his ministerial and teaching career in Thailand and New Zealand.[5] *Waterbuffalo Theology* represents his attempt to work out a theology for Thailand. Its title exemplifies its author's point of view:

> On my way to the country church, I never fail to see a herd of waterbuffaloes grazing in the muddy paddy fields . . . it reminds me that the people to whom I am to bring the gospel of Christ spend most of their time with the waterbuffaloes in the rice field. The waterbuffaloes tell me that I must preach to these farmers in the simplest sentence-structure and thought-development. They remind me to discard all abstract ideas, and to use exclusively objects that are immediately tangible. "Sticky-rice," "banana," "pepper," "dog," "cat," "bicycle," "rainy season" . . . these are meaningful words for them.[6]

Koyama wants to articulate a "rice-roots" theology "from below," one that comes out of the everyday experience of the farmers of northern Thailand. The pace and style of their life are radically different from that of most Westerners. The pace is much slower and the style does not extol efficiency. As Western-imported technology becomes more pervasive, the Thais feel caught between what Koyama calls Thailand One—the traditional—and Thailand Two—the modernized or "busy-business-Thailand." How, then, can the Christian faith speak to the needs of those who live every day at the intersection of the two Thailands? Further, how should they live at the juncture of Buddhism and Christianity? In Koyama's words, "How is the mercy shown in the name of Buddha related to the mercy shown in the name of Jesus Christ?"[7] What is the place of evangelism and worship in a culture which honors both Christ and Buddha?

Koyama uses rich, concrete imagery. For example, he suggests that in order for Christ to appeal to the palates of Thais, theologians must use a proper measure of Aristotelian pepper and Buddhist salt. According to Koyama, Thai theology takes place:

While they [Thais] squat on the dirt ground, and not while sipping tea with missionary friends in the teak-floored shiny living room. When I peep into the kitchen of their theology, the theological situation I see there is unique. No books have been written about this situation and no references are in the best stocked theological libraries![8]

For Koyama, kitchen theology takes precedence over living-room theology, which is another way of saying that indigenous "praxis" theology is prior to missionary "theoretical" theology. For this reason Koyama favors getting rid of mission boards and redefining the missionary as "anyone who increases by participation the concretization of the love of God in history."[9]

In his writings Koyama reveals a special interest in liberating Christians from an imperialistic attitude toward Buddhism and other religions:

I have often been puzzled by missionaries persuading their Asian friends to change their faith from Buddha to Jesus Christ. . . . They themselves are not ready to change one iota of their rigid theological position or denominational security and self-identity. People do not see the *stigma* of Jesus Christ there.[10]

Koyama does not believe that Christianity should be considered superior to other religions. He claims that many Asian Christians share his conviction, but:

I do not think Christianity in Asia for the last four hundred years has really listened to the people. It has ignored the people. It has ignored the spirituality of the people. It has ignored the people's deepest aspiration and frustration.[11]

Koyama makes much use of the concept of idolatry in a manner reminiscent of many Latin American theologians. A religion becomes idolatrous, he asserts, when it tries to put a handle on God, for in so doing it is trying to control God. Koyama is equally critical of the Western idols of speed and efficiency so destructive of the Asian lifestyle. He entitles one of his books *Three Mile An Hour God* to illustrate his point that God works slowly in the conversion process.[12] God's basic educational philosophy is epitomized in the biblical "forty years in the wilderness."[13]

Koyama is in agreement with liberation theologians in South Africa and Latin America in showing a preference for the poor:

The oppressed want justice not charity. The rich want to give charity not justice. In particular, the powerful members of the community want to give "religion" to the poor. "Religion" will take away the complaints of the poor. . . . But God's politics must hear the unuttered cry of one fallen and unable to cry.[14]

In his concern for indigenization, Koyama links arms with many African theologians. In addition, by urging a new and positive relationship between Christianity and Buddhism, Koyama is unveiling a portrait of liberation theology vital to Asia.

Takenaka Masao

Takenaka Masao urges the creation of a new style of living for Asian Christians:

> [A style marked by] a wrestling participation and presence in the concrete place of work and life . . . as the new man who is free and contagiously human within the concrete structure and organisation of society. . . . Wherever there is injustice in society the Christian has a wrestling presence in the situation to restore justice. . . . Wherever misery and exploitation of life exist, he has a wrestling participation in the process of the restoration of humanity in the concrete social context.[15]

Masao believes that out of this participation in the affairs of the world theologians will be able to develop a theology specifically for the Japanese situation.

Toshikazu Takao

Toshikazu Takao points to the influence of the "new-left" students who established the Zenkyoto (All Campus United Struggle Committee) in the late 1960s. The Zenkyoto faulted the universities for failing to discern the ethical implications of the Japanese technological revolution. In their support of the university establishment, these students saw themselves as tools of the oppressor. They began to focus their concerns on such questions as:

> What does the Gospel for the salvation of souls have to do with the new colonialism and the new imperialism? What does the forgiveness of sins have to do with the state monopoly capitalism?[16]

Takao notes that such questions forced the churches to justify their own existence and to ask what their proper role should be in social and political struggles. Some theologians began to realize that theological reflection must start, not from dogmatic premises, but from the realities of human oppression and the need for liberation. Hence, religious priorities had to be reversed, with social liberation becoming the new focus.

CHINA

Little is known about what is happening in Christian theological circles on the Chinese mainland. In the nineteenth century China had been inundated with Christian missioners from the West, an invasion sharply curtailed by the anti-Western Boxer Rebellion at the beginning of the twentieth century. Two of the greatest Chinese leaders in the first half of the twentieth century, Sun Yat-Sen and Chiang Kai-Shek, were Christians, but their religious affiliation did little to stem the rise of anti-Western sentiment. With the communist takeover in 1949, it was imperative that Christianity be reinterpreted in an Asian, pro-Marxist light.

T. C. Chao

Until his death in 1979, T. C. Chao, dean of religion at Yenching University and a former president of the World Council of Churches, openly criticized the close identification that Christianity had maintained with capitalism. He pleaded for a new understanding of Christianity—an avowedly Marxist understanding that would focus on social and economic issues.

Ting Kuang-Hsun

Ting Kuang-Hsun, formerly president of Nanking Seminary, envisages a new understanding of Christianity freed from colonial trappings, an understanding that would identify with the aspirations of the Chinese people. He writes of the new stage of history in which Chinese Christians find themselves:

> [A Stage] of doing away with exploitative systems and of building up socialism in a country which is poor and which has hitherto been semi-colonial and semi-feudalistic.[17]

He faults the Kuomintang and Chiang Kai-Shek for having identified with the oppressor, and suggests that the future goal of Christianity should be to discern the action of God in the historical process of building a new humanity.

HONG KONG

Although Christianity on the Chinese mainland has been heavily influenced by Marxist ideology, this has not been the case in Hong Kong, which remains under strong Western influence. The main sources for creative theological thinking in Hong Kong have been the Tao Fong Shan Ecumenical Centre, its journal *Ching Feng*, and the Industrial Committee of the Hong Kong Christian Council.

Raymond Fung

The Industrial Committee has focused on social injustice in Hong Kong industries. One of its former leaders, Raymond Fung, suggests that Christians should not so much single out the sinner as the one who is "sinned against," the one who is exploited and oppressed. Compassion and liberation become possible only when Christians truly perceive the oppressed as the "sinned against." Fung maintains that the Christian message should be one of "comfort in compassion" to the oppressed and "judgment in compassion" to oppressors.[18]

Peter K. H. Lee

Peter K. H. Lee, director of the Christian Study Center on Chinese Religion and Culture in Hong Kong, notes the profound changes that have taken place in Asia since the Second World War. Asian nations, in their struggle for political independence, have had to face the immense difficulty of reconciling a tradition-bound society with the demands of the oppressed for justice and equality. The gap between rich and poor remains huge, fed in large part by Western multinational corporations. Lee points out that, although most Asian societies have broken away from Western political control, the churches are "still wrapped up in their imperial aura." Siding with the weak against the oppressor must be the first step in church renewal.[19]

TAIWAN

For Taiwan the historical situation is quite different. Japan had occupied Taiwan (Formosa) for fifty years until forced to relinquish it after the Second World War. Under the pro-Western control of the Kuomintang, this country has seen both Catholic and Protestant theologians performing leading roles in the development of an indigenous theology.

Choan-Seng Song

One of the most prominent of Taiwanese Protestant thinkers is Choan-Seng Song. Associate director of the Secretariat of the Faith and Order Commission of the World Council of Churches, Song had previously served as principal of the Taiwan Theological College.

Song's liveliest contribution is *Third-Eye Theology*.[20] His basic contention is that theology should begin with the heart that transcends reason and is a window to the mystery of Being. The heart serves as a "third eye," a visual image that Song borrows from the Japanese Zen master Daisetz Suzuki:

> Zen . . . wants us to open a "third eye," as Buddhists call it, to the hitherto unheard-of region shut away from us through our own ignorance. When the cloud of ignorance disappears, the infinity of heaven is manifested where we see for the first time into the nature of our own being.[21]

Christians in Asia, Song maintains, must learn to see Christ through Asian eyes. This approach is more intuitive than conceptual, more heartfelt than rational. The mission of the church is to inform "the Asian spirituality shaped by Asian cultures and religions with the love of God in Jesus Christ."[22]

Song also speaks of a "theology of the womb," a theology of liberation that leads to a new life struggling to come into existence:

> As a mother commits herself totally to bringing into fruition the seed of life within her, so Christians must be committed to the emergence of a new world in which light prevails over darkness, love overcomes hate, and freedom vanquishes oppression.[23]

Song displays an intimate knowledge of Latin American liberation theology and uses the exodus theme to point to God's participation in the political process. Like his counterparts in Latin America, he insists:

> What is historical is political. This basic understanding of the relationship between history and politics is essential for the Christian churches in Asia today as they try to wrestle with the political implications of the Christian faith.[24]

Also in concert with his Latin American counterparts, he stresses that oppressors, as well as the oppressed, are in need of liberation.

In subsequent writings, Song develops what he calls "Chuang-tzu theology." He contends that just as Chuang-tzu tried to perceive the nature of reality from the perspective of fish and butterfly, so too should Christians seek to transcend the boundaries of history, religion, and culture to develop deeper contacts with the mysterious ways in which God deals with nature and human nature:

> Such a theology calls for a sensitivity that can respond creatively to vibrations coming from the depth of the human spirit outside the familiar realm of everyday life.[25]

In *The Tears of Lady Meng*, Song presents a parable for a political theology.[26] Lady Meng, in her agony and tears, redeems the brutal death of her husband by denouncing the wicked emperor and sacrificing her own life. Similarly, the Asian oppressed who, with Jesus and the Buddha, also weep, must find in their own experience the resources that will unite them in their struggle against injustice.

One of Song's unique contributions is his use of parables to suggest new ways of doing theology. His *Tell Us Our Names: Story Theology from an Asian Perspective* is a compendium of folktales and fairy stories from different parts of the world.[27] He uses them to suggest how Christians should reinterpret their faith in a pluralistic world, for, as he contends, one task of Third World theology is that of helping traditional churches enlarge their vision of God's mission.

Song also maintains that the concept of liberation must include the liberation of history from narrow religious interests. History must no longer be cut to pieces by Christians, Buddhists, Jews, and others, because "no religious system, however great, can contain God."[28] In urging this broadened understanding of history, Song is pointing to one more feature of the sin of idolatry that looms so large in the thinking of Kosuke Koyama and Latin American liberation theologians.

SRI LANKA

Sri Lanka, formerly called Ceylon, has had a long tradition of twin cultures: Sinhalese Buddhism and Tamil Hinduism. This heritage has been deeply eroded by the colonial control of the Dutch and Portuguese in the sixteenth and seventeenth centuries, and by England, which exerted power from the eighteenth century until 1948 when Sri Lanka gained its independence. Since 1948 Sri Lanka has seen a resurgence of both Buddhism and Hinduism that has forced the Christian churches to rid themselves of Western trappings and create new forms more germane to its Asian context.

A great Sri Lankan Christian leader of recent date was D.T. Niles. A prolific writer and speaker, Niles served as chairman of the World Student Christian Federation, secretary of the World YMCA, and member of the Faith and Order Commission of the World Council of Churches. For many Christians he was the incarnation of the ecumenical movement.

The indigenization of Christianity in Sri Lanka was bolstered by the establishment of the Ecumenical Institute for Study and Dialogue in 1963. Other organizations that played a significant role were the National Christian Council, the Student Christian Movement, and, in particular, the Centre for Society and Religion.

Tissa Balasuriya

Tissa Balasuriya, who heads the Centre for Society and Religion, has been perhaps the most influential Sri Lankan theologian, and *The Eucharist and Human Liberation* is one of his most widely-read works.[29] In it he develops what he calls an action-oriented liturgy, focusing on the efforts of the oppressed to achieve their own liberation. An authentic liturgy for today must reflect such themes as food, clothing, shelter, health, work, family, justice, and religious harmony—basic exigencies of the everyday lives of the oppressed. The Eucharist should have as its purpose the building of a new world order based on equality, service, and justice. Whereas the liturgy has traditionally been geared toward individual salvation, in the future it must be directed toward the fundamental concerns of the social order.

Balasuriya considers the profit motive behind capitalism incompatible with the spirit of the Eucharist; he suggests instead a form of socialism in which there is common ownership of the means of production and distribution:

While there are often sharp divergences between Christians and Marxists, there is also a very deep interconnection. . . . Marxism can teach Christians what the Eucharist must mean in the real world of class exploitation. Christians can recall Marxists to the ideal of the classless society in which human beings must all be respected in equality and freedom.[30]

But Balasuriya's espousal of a form of socialism does not mean that he fails to recognize potential dangers and defects in a socialist society. Quite the contrary. Both socialist and capitalist societies can misuse their share of wealth. Balasuriya maintains that what is needed today is a drastic rethinking of the proper use of economic resources on a global rather than on a national basis. Balasuriya criticizes Latin American liberation theologians for their lack of a world vision of economic matters:

Does Latin American theology, while basing itself on social analysis, consider seriously the causes and effects of present-day problems in Iran, Afghanistan, Vietnam, Kampuchea, South Africa, etc.? How do your analyses of capitalist and socialist societies understand these global conflicts? . . . We would like to see your theology develop in the direction of more practical international cooperation with efforts of the people in the Third World to restructure the world economic system.[31]

Along this same line Balasuriya also faults Latin American liberation theologians for putting too much emphasis on socio-economic factors and too little on the role that land itself plays in economic development:

The principal obstacle to economic development is not merely lack of capital, technology, or organizational ability. Rather it is the relationship between people and land. Land is the main resource base for human living. The present national frontiers, set up by the European takeover of the earth, are the main impediment to human beings going to the vast land space of the planet. Land hunger or land acquisition is the main cause of international wars.[32]

In his writings Balasuriya also addresses the need for Christianity to be liberated from its traditional, parochial attitude toward other religions:

As an Asian I cannot accept as divine and true any teaching which begins with the presupposition that all my ancestors for innumerable generations are eternally damned by God unless they had been baptized in or were related to one of the Christian institutional churches. . . . Theology must honestly respect these millions upon millions of my ancestors and future human beings before I can accept theology as a true interpretation of revelation from a loving God.[33]

Balasuriya believes that theology itself needs to be liberated—liberated from Western culture, from church centralization, from male clerical domination, from a procapitalist, anticommunist bias.

If one were to read only one book in the area of Asian liberation theology, let it be Tissa Balasuriya's *Planetary Theology*.[34] Here he criticizes liberation theologies for being too contextual and limited, thus preventing them from developing a universal perspective. Marginalized racial groups, for example, receive scant attention from Latin American liberation theologians and African black theology overlooks the needs of Asians. Furthermore, most forms of Third World liberation theology have been seriously remiss concerning the oppression of women. Balasuriya insists that every contextual theology should recognize that there is "world apartheid"[35] and that it comes in many shapes and sizes:

> We are called on to transcend our narrow particularities in order to arrive at a higher, wider, and deeper level of sharing among all human beings. This calls for a transformation of ourselves from within our innermost being to accept all others as sisters and brothers. Our growth to a planetary dimension is an invitation to spiritual deepening, a purification from selfishness to a more universal communion in real life, to our own humanization. Insofar as we do so, we shall become truly civilized, approach the ideals of the best in all our religions and cultures, and pursue the deepest and best aspiration of every human heart and mind.[36]

Balasuriya sets forth the notion of the liberator God to develop what he calls an ecumenism of all religions, a God who combats all forms of injustice on a global basis. He also believes in a cosmic Christ whose core message is one of "integral liberation—of the person, of society, and of the world in truth, authenticity, social justice, and peace."[37] Balasuriya here points the way to a new, expanded liberation theology that will embrace all cultures, religions, and societies.

Aloysius Pieris

Another Sri Lankan theologian who articulates the theme of liberation as it pertains to the relationships among the religions of the world is Aloysius Pieris. Director of the Centre for Research and Dialogue at Kelaniza, Pieris believes that Asian Christians should come to terms with the irruption of the non-Christian world by expanding the existing boundaries of orthodoxy. Pieris criticizes some Latin American liberation theologians—he singles out Jon Sobrino—for promoting a christology that pits Christ against other religions. This Western colonial view Pieris finds totally unacceptable in the context of Asian multifaceted religiosity. Pieris suggests a "Christ-of-religions" approach in which persons of all religious traditions might unite in a quest for liberation from all forms of oppression: political, social, economic, racial, sexual, and spiritual.[38] On this point he and his fellow countryman Tissa Balasuriya are in full agreement.[39]

THE PHILIPPINES

The history of the Philippines, like that of other Asian countries, includes a recurring pattern of foreign invasion and domination. From the sixteenth through the nineteenth centuries, Spain served as the overlord in the Philippines. In the twentieth century, the United States took over the Spanish role, with Japan temporarily replacing the United States during the Second World War.

With the arrival of Ferdinand Magellan in 1521, Christian missionaries started their work of "converting the heathen." By the early seventeenth century, a majority of the inhabitants were Catholic. Today 85 percent of the population is Catholic. Since the 1920s, Catholic and Protestant theologians initiated efforts to construct an indigenous Filipino theology, but their efforts bore little fruit until the achievement of political independence after the Second World War. By the 1960s, Christian leaders exhibited increasing concern about the social and economic injustices so deeply rooted in their country, but the imposition of martial law by President Marcos in 1972 made the exercise of their concerns much more difficult. Yet, despite this setback, struggle has continued in such movements as Christians for National Liberation and the Civil Liberties Union.

Edicio de la Torre

Edicio de la Torre, one of the founders of the Christians for National Liberation, has been particularly vocal in stressing the relationship between Christianity and Maoism. Often jailed for his outspokenness, la Torre has urged Filipino Christians to consider Maoism as a viable political alternative:

> To take the challenge of Marxism seriously is to take the Incarnation in Philippine society seriously: to concretely analyze concrete situations and to side with the oppressed people in their struggle for liberation, not as a self-appointed leader but as a servant of the revolution.[40]

Levi V. Oracion

Levi V. Oracion, vice-president for theological education in the Philippine Christian University, Manila, insists that Christianity should show a preference for the poor:

The outcasts of society have been granted [by Jesus] the privilege of being the first citizens of God's Kingdom, and the high and the mighty may enter the Kingdom only if they give themselves in service to the poor.[41]

Oracion believes that basic human rights are rooted in God's righteousness: hence, to oppress any human being is to oppress God. The primary task of the church is to make known God's radical opposition to human injustice.

Francisco F. Claver

Francisco F. Claver, retired bishop of Bukidnon in the Philippines and a member of the Bontoc Igorot tribe, is widely known for his protests against the repressive regime of President Marcos. Claver believes that Christ's central mission is to liberate the poor and that this mission precludes any separation of church and politics. Indeed, there may be times when violence is morally justifiable, especially when the weak are being trampled upon by the strong. Claver advocates what he calls "the violence of the meek," a strategy for political action in which "the lowly" conscientize and liberate themselves through their own courageous involvement in political affairs.[42]

Carlos H. Abesamis

Carlos H. Abesamis, coordinator of the Justice and Peace Department of the National Secretariat of Social Action, Manila, is engaged in developing a theology centering on a full-fledged commitment to the struggles of the Asian oppressed. He maintains that theologians should be grass-roots Christians, and he argues that every theology is conditioned by the class position and consciousness of its originator.

To be sure, Abesamis agrees that Asians need to be liberated from American and European models of theology. But of equal importance is the need to be liberated from the theology of the Asian middle class. If the grass-roots poor refuse to do their own theologizing, it would be better for the middle class to maintain a respectful silence than to muddy the theological waters:

But even now, there already exist nuggets of a new theology embedded, certainly not in the learned periodicals of the contemporary ruling theology, but in the prayers shared by the grassroots poor among themselves at their sessions, in their creative liturgy, drama and songs, in their story-telling and attempts at poem-writing: all indicators to us of a new religious culture in the living journal of our people's lives.[43]

Abesamis reaffirms the basic contention of Latin American liberation theologians, that theology must be grounded in the daily experiences of grass-roots communities. The most that middle-class Asian theologians can do is to assist in the transitional process in which "grass-roots theologians" will take over and middle-class theologians fade away!

Emerito P. Nacpil

Emerito P. Nacpil, dean of the South East Asia Graduate School of Theology and executive director of the Association of Theological Schools in South East Asia, has shown special concern for the vast social changes that the process of modernization has caused in southern Asia—a process Kosuke Koyama refers to in his discussion of "Thailand Two." For Nacpil, the church must respond creatively to this process and become an agent for social innovation and the development of a new humanity. He suggests three dimensions of a liberation theology for the Philippines: the gospel as liberation from oppression, as summons to responsibility, and as horizon of hope. Here we see a clear parallel between Nacpil and Gustavo Gutiérrez in the threefold nature of liberation. Nacpil suggests:

> If the new Filipino is seeking deliverance from the past and freedom for the future, if he is seeking liberation from the gods and spirits, and freedom to change the world: then the Christian Gospel is indeed "good news" for him. It is the Gospel for the new Filipino.[44]

Ben Dominguez

Ben Dominguez, professor of the New Testament at the Union Theological Seminary in Manila, has shown particular interest in uncovering the religious and cultural heritage of Asia—a heritage no longer to be considered "sub-Christian," but fully authentic and rich in its own right.[45]

C. G. Arevalo

Professor of eschatology and theology at the Loyola School of Theology in Manila and a member of the Pontifical International Theological Commission, C. G. Arevalo applauds the development of Latin American liberation theology and urges a similar approach for the Asian oppressed. For Arevalo, human rights must be at the top of the agenda:

> The only authentic response to the one true God is not the religious one, but the human struggle on the side of the poor and the oppressed. . . . Surely here we have a christology "from below" (with a vengeance!) which is almost wholly functional to liberation theology and liberation spirituality as well.[46]

These words could just as well have come from virtually any Latin American or South African liberation theologian.

Charles Avila

A seasoned organizer of peasant unions, Charles Avila is the former vice-president of the Federation of Free Farmers. In addition to his activities in behalf of the poor and oppressed, he made a major contribution to liberation theology by uncovering attitudes toward landownership among the church fathers. His *Ownership: Early Christian Teaching* is a careful compilation of the teachings on ownership by Clement of Alexandria, Origen, John Chrysostom, Ambrose, Augustine, and many others.[47] All of them support the view of the peasantry of the Third World today, a peasantry seeking "liberation from landlordism and corporate farming" and seeking the kind of justice in which "humanity has effectively rejected the idolatry of property."[48] Avila's book is important for showing how from earliest times the Christian gospel has shown "a preference for the poor" that incorporates the notion of ownership based exclusively on a conscientious stewardship vis-à-vis God-given natural resources.

INDIA

Christianity was first transplanted to India by the Nestorians in the fourth century. Later, Catholic missionaries came in the wake of the Portuguese and French colonization of India, with Protestant missionaries accompanying the British in the seventeenth century. Yet, unlike Christianity in the Philippines, Indian Christians have been and remain a small minority surrounded by a dominant Hindu culture.

One of the earliest pioneers in Christian missions was the Jesuit Roberto de Nobili. Arriving in the city of Madura in southern India in 1607, de Nobili adopted the ascetic practices so much a part of Brahmanic Hinduism and was called a "Roman Brahman" by his Hindu admirers. His controversial methods won the approval of Pope Gregory XV in 1623, and for the remainder of his life he was a religious pilgrim walking and preaching throughout southern India, urging a faith that combined the highest moral and social insights of Hinduism and Christianity.

By the beginning of the twentieth century Indian Christian leaders were making greater attempts to encourage positive relationships between Hindus and Christians, an effort fueled later in no small measure by the Hindu Mahatma Gandhi's praise of Jesus as one of the great spiritual leaders of all time. Christian leaders such as C. F. Andrews and S. K. George saw in Gandhi an authentic manifestation of Christian love. Later Paul Devanandan, the founder of the Christian Institute for the Study of Religion and Society, spoke of the Spirit as being manifest in both Hindu and Christian traditions. During the past two decades many Indian Christian theologians have become involved in the struggle for economic and social justice.

Samuel Rayan

Samuel Rayan, professor and dean at the Vidyajoti Institute in Delhi, has sought to implement in India the reforms promoted by the Vatican Council of the early 1960s, while trying to develop an indigenous theology of liberation. Rayan believes that to take the justice of God seriously means to overcome all forms of human oppression. The central mission of Jesus is to encourage persons to take charge of their own destinies and to free themselves from ritual morality and religion. For this reason, the church must be particularly sensitive to the plight of the poor:

> The concern of the church is not Christians but the poor; its struggle is not for itself but for the liberation of all men and women who are held captive. . . . The task of the church is to champion a whole new social order.[49]

Truth, Rayan contends, does not mean words and dogma. Truth is persons, especially the poor. A theology of, by, and for the poor should be our first priority. Rayan is deeply sensitive to the immense poverty of the masses existing alongside the enormous wealth of the privileged few. He knows how the caste system and tribal patterns have perpetuated this yawning chasm. He suggests:

> There is a growing perception that Hinduism without caste is as possible and desirable as Christianity without hierarchy, even if what emerges in the process will be different from the Hinduism and the Christianity we have known, provided they are in touch with the people whom God loves and liberates. There are attempts to go to the roots and origins of religious heritage to draw inspiration for the struggle for the humanization of our history. These sources may be Hindu, Christian, Muslim, or Buddhist. They are not in conflict as long as they are for human wholeness.[50]

K. Matthew Kurian

K. Matthew Kurian, director of the Institute for Regional Development Studies in Kerala, has written extensively about the decline of capitalism and the rise of socialism in Asia today. He faults the multinational corporations for threatening the political and economic independence of Asian countries, as well as for doing nothing about the abject poverty in which 85 percent of the population of Asia continues to live. He points out that capitalist countries today suffer from unemployment, poverty, and inflation, whereas socialist countries exhibit rising standards of living for workers and their families.[51]

Sebastian Kappen

Sebastian Kappen, director of the Centre for Social Reconstruction, Madras, believes that we encounter God today primarily in the process of building a new social order based on freedom for everyone. Indeed, for Kappen "there is no other way that the divine can appear to human beings." The cosmic, social, and historical dimensions of life cannot be separated. Unlike the spirituality of the West, Asian spirituality has had the native genius to keep all the dimensions of life intertwined. Kappen believes that concern for the well-being of the poor is an important expression of spirituality, and one in which all persons of good will can unite. In fact, Kappen insists that if an authentic Asian liberation theology does emerge, it will probably emanate from dissenting Christians who are willing to "join hands with people of other religions or even with Marxists."[52]

Samuel Amirtham

Professor at the Tamilnadu Theological Seminary, Samuel Amirtham is another Indian theologian who maintains that the primary mission of the church today should be an uncompromising demand for religious and social justice. Because the church may not have any special expertise in solving these social problems, it should ally itself with other agencies and individuals, including non-Christian groups and individuals, in confronting these problems for, after all, God's people are not only Christians! "All those who are oppressed all over the world and are being liberated are, in a sense, Harijans, God's people."[53]

Geevarghese Mar Osthathios

Geevarghese Mar Osthathios, metropolitan of the Orthodox Syrian Church of Kerala, South India, uses his own Orthodox tradition to show the social implications of the doctrine of the Trinity. He insists that "any true Christian theology is a theology of a classless society."[54] He is also convinced that authentic Christianity is easier to practice in a socialist than in a capitalist society:

> God, who chose Cyrus the heathen to fulfill his plans about Israel, was gracious enough to choose Karl Marx, Engels and Mao Tse-Tung to fulfill his plan to evolve a classless society.[55]

To be sure, socialism, like any other "ism," is not immune to corruption, yet Mar Osthathios believes that a society with no class distinctions has a better chance of eliminating injustice than does a capitalist society. Mar Osthathios has strong objections to many facets of communism—in particular, its determinism, materialism, atheism, and lack of individual freedom. But he praises communism for its nationalization of the means of production, its principle of social equality, and its elimination of inherent class distinctions. In this respect the Church must do its part in promoting a simpler lifestyle and in breaking down the economic and social barriers between the rich and poor, oppressors and oppressed.

J. R. Chandran

Principal of the United Theological College in Bangalore, J. R. Chandran warns against absolutizing any ideology, including Marxism, as the best instrument for promoting social justice:

Even though Marxism has contributed more than any other ideology to contemporary struggles for justice, we must be aware of the possibility that a Marxist fundamentalism could betray the cause of liberation of the oppressed.[56]

For this reason every ideology and social program must be scrutinized again and against lest it betray the struggles of the oppressed for liberation. Moreover, inasmuch as the Third World itself exhibits so much diversity, we should expect and welcome the emergence of a variety of liberation theologies based on different social ideologies.

Stanley J. Samartha

Stanley J. Samartha, director of the WCC program on Dialogue with People of Living Faiths and Ideologies, sums up the new attitude toward other religions:

There is no reason to claim that the religion developed in the desert around Mount Sinai is superior to the religion developed on the banks of the River Ganga.[57]

Samartha suggests a christology for India centering on the struggles of the Indian people for freedom from all forms of bondage—a christology not to be identified with any particular theology and one large enough to encompass the entire human family. At this point Samartha is in full accord with Aloysius Pieris of Sri Lanka in opting for a cosmic view of Christ that transcends historical religions.[58]

INDONESIA

Indonesia has been a major meeting ground for Hindu, Buddhist, Muslem, and Christian cultures, with Muslems today forming the vast majority. Nevertheless, Christianity has deep roots in Indonesia; after the Dutch arrived early in the seventeenth century, the Dutch Reformed Church became virtually the state church. The Second World War saw the Japanese take over and when, after the war, Indonesia achieved independence, the Indonesian Christian Council performed an important role in the struggle for human rights.

Henriette Marianne Katoppo

A leading advocate of the development of a theology indigenous to Indonesia, one that would include full rights for women and minority groups, is Henriette Marianne Katoppo. A graduate of Jakarta Theological Seminary and an active participant in the Indonesian Student Christian Movement, Katoppo's major book to date is *Compassionate and Free: An Asian Woman's Theology.*[59] She contends in this work that to be a Christian in Asia has traditionally meant to be a European Christian, because Asian forms of religious expression were denounced as pagan. Katoppo's primary aim is to forge "an Asian women's theology." Eschewing the phrase "feminist theology" because it has become "too loaded," she explains that the purpose of her theology is to raise the crucial question, How do Asians encounter God? She answers her question in terms of her own experience:

> I found that to be the Other was an alienating experience: the Christian among the Muslims, the westernized Minahassan who was out of place in a Japanese society, the girl who was taught to look upon boys as equals, not superiors.[60]

For Katoppo, the purpose of theology is to make the experience of the Other a liberating, not an alienating, condition. In so doing, liberation becomes a real possibility for women as well as for men. In her development of an Asian women's theology, Katoppo stresses how important it is for women *and* men to work together in the building of a just society.

Katoppo considers the Virgin Mary an important role model for women. Mary is truly compassionate and free, because she gave herself completely to God. Mary's virginity refers to an inner quality, that of "the liberated human being who—not being subject to any other human being—is free to serve God."[61] In her affirmation of Mary as the ideal symbol for the autonomy of women—that is, Mary is the one who does not lead a *derived* life ("mother of," "wife of," etc.)—Katoppo, the Protestant, is critical of Gustavo Gutiérrez, the Catholic, for his neglect of Mary in his own theology of liberation:

> It speaks for itself that Gutiérrez, the famous liberation theologian . . . makes little mention of Mary although the Magnificat is generally attributed to her. Is this perhaps an example of the way women are constantly eclipsed in history—this occurring so often and so naturally that we simply forget that things should be different?[62]

Katoppo also suggests that if we can read the Bible without its masculine bias, we shall discover underlying female imagery. We shall discover, for example, that Yahweh is neither male nor female, and that service, not sexuality, is the primary reflection of God's image. Like C. S. Song, Katoppo uses the metaphor "theology of the womb" to dramatize the continuation of life, of kinship, and of a sense of hope from one generation to the next.

Albert Widjaja

Albert Widjaja, lecturer in economics at the Institute Oikumene Indonesia, makes an important contribution to liberation theology in distinguishing between "theological begging" and "beggarly theology." The former term refers to the tendency to borrow from and imitate other theologians as if their theologies represented the normative interpretation of the Christian faith:

> The practice of theological begging has been one of the major outcomes of the western missionary endeavour. And it is not least promoted by the western seminary theologians, who educated the church leaders of the third world.[63]

On the other hand, "beggarly theology" is to be understood in the spirit of the beggar:

> The true spirit of the beggar can be discovered when he encounters a garbage container. He faces the garbage with a sense of anticipation. He believes that something will come out as invaluable, even though the garbage as a whole is considered junk by society.[64]

Beggarly theology identifies with the poor and dispossessed. It demands that the claims of the Christian gospel be linked with the cries of the oppressed. Widjaja believes it to be a mature theology in that it does not depend on other established theologies—the begging approach—but rather becomes responsible for its own development in the context of Asian realities. Widjaja's notion of beggarly theology shows a strong correlation with the main focus of Latin American liberation theology and its concern for the poor and dispossessed.

SOUTH KOREA

For centuries Korea has been the target of foreign intrusion, especially by China and Japan. Although the Yi dynasty was in power in Korea from the fifteenth century until the early part of the twentieth century, during this period Korea was usually under the domination of China or Japan, with Japan ruling Korea continuously from 1876 to 1945.

Catholic missionaries first arrived in Korea in 1784, followed by Protestant missionaries in 1884. Korean Christianity has always contained many elements of Buddhism, Confucianism, and the native shamanistic tradition. In the 1920s and 1930s, many younger Korean theologians, Presbyterians in particular, were educated in Japan and began to sense the need for an indigenous theology free from Western influence. With the partitioning of Korea in the early 1950s, the Presbyterian Church, Republic of Korea, was established, under the leadership of Kim Jai-Jin. He was highly influential in laying the groundwork for the development of a Korean liberation theology that has often been at odds with the government. Urban programs sponsored by the Urban Industrial Mission, the Korea Student Mission Movement, and the YMCA have also been powerful forces in relating the Christian faith to the struggle for genuine democracy and social justice.

In 1973 a document entitled *The Theological Declaration of Korean Christians* was widely circulated, despite government opposition. This document was a voice for liberation theology in demanding the eradication of social injustice and affirming the ultimate victory of the oppressed. Government opposition to these stirrings of liberation increased in the late 1970s, but theological voices of protest against government oppression continued to be heard, some of whom will be mentioned here.

Kim Chung-Choon

Kim Chung-Choon, professor of Old Testament studies at Hankuk Seminary, suggests that God is to be found most profoundly in the midst of human suffering. Like so many liberation theologians, he points to the exodus as a key liberation event for God's own involvement in the human struggle. He suggests:

> God hears the human cryings and groanings from the place of struggle all over the world. The cry of the drowning Boat People from South Asia; the cry of the rejected and discriminated people from the lands of racism; the cry of the mistreated and exploited from the lands of rapidly developing countries under dictatorship; the cry of the poor and alienated people from the lands of capitalism; and the cry of the imprisoned and rejected people from the land where one political ideology, like communism, is dominant and oppressive.[65]

Kim Chung-Choon believes it important for Christians today to reap the rich insights of the Korean shamanistic tradition. The role of the shaman is to appease the spirits of the dead. Kim Chung-Choon sees a parallel here with God's support of the legitimate cries of the oppressed: "We Christians should be the Shamans of Christ, full of the Holy Spirit . . . identifying ourselves with suffering humanity."[66]

The Korean notion of *han*, meaning the accumulation of grief and oppression, also has implications for Christians:

The ministry of the Church must accent the appeasement of "Han," so that all the rejected, despised, imprisoned, exploited, alienated and the poor may have joy and satisfaction.[67]

The most significant theological development in Korea in recent years has been minjung theology. (The minjung are the oppressed and downtrodden: those who have no rights.) This movement emerged primarily from individuals involved in the Urban Industrial Mission in the 1970s and their struggle for basic human rights.

Kim Yong-Bok

A leading spokesman of minjung theology is Kim Yong-Bok, codirector of the Christian Institute for Justice and Development in Seoul. He understands the meaning of minjung in this way:

Woman belongs to minjung when she is politically dominated by men. An ethnic group is a minjung group when it is politically dominated by another group. A race is minjung when it is dominated by another powerful ruling race. When intellectuals are suppressed by the military power elite, they belong to minjung. Of course, the same applies to the workers and farmers.[68]

Who, then, are the minjung? Kim Yong-Bok replies:

They are the have-nots. They are farmers, fisherman, laborers, unemployed, soldiers, policemen, salesmen, small shopkeepers, small producers. They suffer political suppression, economic exploitation, social humiliation and cultural alienation.[69]

Kim Yong-Bok sees the minjung as the subjects of history in the development of a new historical consciousness that can lead to the birth of a new community of liberated human beings.

Like much of African theology, minjung theology seeks a creative relationship between Christianity and its indigenous Korean setting. For example, the Korean God Hananim, traceable to shamanistic tradition, is considered to be the chief of all spirits. Although Hananim's influence was usually considered minimal in the daily lives of the Korean people, Hananim took on greater importance when Christians co-opted Hananim as the Lord of history.

Suh Nam-Dong

Another minjung theologian is Suh Nam-Dong, formerly professor of systematic theology at Yonsei University. Suh Nam-Dong interprets the Korean concept of *han* to be the underlying feeling of the Korean people; it includes both despair and hope. *Han* is the language of the minjung, the oppressed who, despite their cries of anguish and despair, still hope and continue to work for a new humanity. Suh Nam-Dong believes that Korean theologians should stop dwelling on doctrinal discussions and concentrate instead on developing *han* as the new dominant theological theme.[70]

Kim Chi-Ha

Kim Chi-Ha is one of the best known poets in Korea. Acknowledging the great influence that the Korean Christian Movement for Democratic Rights had on his own life (he was converted to Catholicism in 1971), Kim Chi-Ha is deeply interested in placing the Christian faith, and the figure of Jesus in particular, in a Korean setting. Often tortured and imprisoned, Kim Chi-Ha also sees the importance of articulating a theology of the minjung.[71]

In his story "The Gold-Crowned Jesus," Kim Chi-Ha depicts Jesus as an inert figure of gold, imprisoned in concrete by his oppressor. A leper, the symbol of the oppressed, wants to liberate Jesus from imprisonment. He removes the gold crown from Jesus' head and asks him how his, Jesus', liberation can be accomplished. Jesus replies:

> My power alone is not enough. People like you must help to liberate me. Those who seek only the comforts, wealth, honor, and power of this world, who wish entry to the kingdom of heaven for themselves only and ignore the poor and less fortunate, cannot give me life again. Neither can those who have never suffered loneliness, who remain silent while injustice is done and so acquiesce in it, who are without courage. . . . It is the same with those without courage who are unwilling to resist such evildoers as dictators, and other tyrants who inflict great suffering on the weak and poor. Prayer alone is not enough; it is necessary also to act. Only those, though very poor and suffering like yourself, who are generous in spirit and seek to help the poor and wretched can give me life again. You removed the gold crown from my head and so freed my lips to speak. People like you will be my liberators.[72]

But in the end the leper fails to liberate Christ. He is compelled by the forces of oppression in both state and church to restore the gold crown to Jesus' head, thereby imprisoning him once again.

Korean minjung theology is particularly important for its creative combination of the two chief features of liberation theology in the Third World. On the one hand, it is a theology growing out of the grass roots—the minjung—in their struggle for liberation. On the other hand, it seeks to relate itself to the indigenous Korean setting, incorporating the shamanistic tradition in a constructive way.[73]

Asian liberation theology is a rapidly growing, multifaceted phenomenon similar in its basic aspirations to African and Latin American liberation theology, yet distinctive in its pluralistic religious setting.[74] One should not even begin to speak with a shred of confidence about the "pros and cons" of Third World liberation theology until one gains some degree of sensitivity to and appreciation for its multiple Asian versions. Asian liberation theology is original, complex, rich, bewildering, and immensely fertile. It provides important models for liberation, not only for the Third World, but also for the First World.

COLLEGE FOR HUMAN SERVICES
LIBRARY
345 HUDSON STREET
NEW YORK, NY 10014

CHAPTER FIVE

Liberation Theology and its Critics

Throughout the preceding survey one characteristic of Third World liberation theology has become increasingly more obvious: there can be no single overarching liberation theology, for the obvious reason that historical situations differ vastly in Asia, Africa, and Latin America. Anyone interested in understanding and evaluating Third World liberation theology must be on guard against simplistic caricatures. For example, it is imprudent to judge African and Asian forms of liberation theology in terms of Latin American models. The reason for this is twofold. First, to make Latin American liberation theology *the* norm entails an elitism to which African and Asian theologians have rightfully objected.

Secondly, Latin American liberation theology itself manifests a wide-ranging variety of interpretation: Gutiérrez, Alves, Miranda, Sobrino, Couch, and others. Yet an evaluation of African and Asian theology in the light of criteria taken from the "Latin American experience" is perhaps the most common error made by both friends and foes of liberation theology. With these warnings in mind, I want to focus attention on several major criticisms frequently directed at Third World liberation theology.

"THE GOSPEL DEEMPHASIZED"

Liberation theology is criticized for so overstressing the historical setting that the Christian gospel gets lost in the shuffle. As one critic, Bonaventure Kloppenburg, puts it:

> The theologian who uses the situation as his starting point must not forget that, like the Church, he is not above the Word (which includes doctrine, without which the Word would be empty), but at its service.[1]

Another critic, W. Dayton Roberts, maintains that "the hero of the theology of liberation seems to fit Judas Maccabaeus better than Jesus of Nazareth."[2]

Both observers are correct in their contention that Third World liberation theology begins with a particular historical situation, and applies what Phillip

100

Berryman calls the "Medellín method" of reflection upon that situation. Theological and pastoral conclusions derive from this reflection.[3] A problem arises if—as Kloppenburg and Roberts charge—the gospel becomes a secondary concern for liberation theologians.

Third World liberation theologians would vehemently reject this charge. They would insist that the Christian faith is as important to them as it is to their critics. They might refer to the two-pronged approach of Karl Barth, who used to say that he would read with the newspaper in one hand and the Bible in the other. Liberation theologians merely replace the newspaper with present living conditions of the poor and oppressed.

To be sure, putting the historical context—or one's own particular theological preference, for that matter—on a par with the Christian faith runs the risk of reading into the gospel and the Bible what one wants to find there.[4] Few theologians evade this temptation. In his perceptive article, "Karl Barth and Liberation Theology," George Hunsinger notes how Barth and liberation theologians read the Bible differently because their approaches to scripture are different. Barth's attachment to God's word means that:

> Theology reads Scripture, and especially its narrative portions, as an organic whole. Scripture will be regarded as possessing its own integrity despite all diversity, its own complex logic, and its own canons of meaning and truth. . . . How could it be otherwise when the Word to which theology bears witness is utterly unique?[5]

By the same token liberation theologians' attachment to the conditions of the poor and oppressed means that:

> Scripture will be read as the story of God's liberation of the oppressed, and its exegesis will take place in deeds. The deed will be what counts, and so orthodoxy will be supplanted by orthopraxis. How could it be otherwise when God has initiated a process of liberation whose goal will be the creation of a new humanity and in which theology is called to participate in solidarity with the oppressed?[6]

There are a plurality of interpretations of the Bible just as there are a plurality of traditions in the churches. One's interpretation of the Bible and of the Christian faith will always be limited and to some extent self-serving. This becomes a problem only if one insists that one's own interpretation must be normative for others. One can thus question José Miranda's assertion that the New Testament explicitly teaches communism. It is true that certain passages he selects suggest communism—defined as the equal sharing of goods in common ownership—but communism is not the one and only biblical perspective.

If the views of Third World liberation theologians are carefully examined, it will be found that they take their Christian convictions very seriously; they do not treat them as a secondary consideration or as an ex post facto rationalization of a given political stance. In fact, these theologians are far more conservative theologically than the "death of God" theologians of the 1960s, who not only denied the existence of God, but recast Jesus into a secular saint. No Third World liberation theologian has been guilty of either of these charges. Gutiérrez grounds his call for the liberation of the oppressed in scripture; he sees the exodus and resurrection events as pivotal points in the action of the liberator God. Gutiérrez's *We Drink from Our Own Wells* is a vigorous defense of a spirituality of liberation rooted in Christ and the Bible. Leonardo Boff points to Christ as the "liberator of the human condition." Jon Sobrino insists that the way to justice and liberation is through witnessing to Christ. Segundo Galilea suggests a "liberation spirituality" linking the religious and political realms.

Third World liberation theologians speak with one voice when they insist that the Christian faith is not a by-product of the historical situation, but entails a constant interaction between creed and life. To be sure, any theology that takes its historical context seriously runs the risk of distorting the faith. Liberation theologians, like all other theologians, need to be aware of this danger.

But surely the critics of liberation theology who complain that it puts too much emphasis on the historical context must admit that historical contexts differ. Korea is different from Europe. Thailand is different from Peru. South Africa is different from Sri Lanka. The historical context is of absolute importance in framing and concretizing the content of the Christian faith. How could it be otherwise?

"REFLECTION DISDAINED"

A second criticism, closely related to the first, is that liberation theology, in its emphasis on the historical context, loses sight of the ontological and transcendent dimensions of theology. Critics fault liberation theologians for emphasizing action over reflection, the existential over the speculative, doing over knowing, the practical over the theoretical, and immanence over transcendence. One such critic, Schubert Ogden, has called attention to the liberation theologians' neglect of the ontological. He contends that liberation theology is more witness than theology: it pays undue attention to the existential meaning of God at the expense of God's "metaphysical being."[7]

Third World liberation theologians obviously see the matter differently. They are extremely wary of setting up what they consider to be an artificial distinction between action and reflection, the immanent and the transcendent, and so on. They view reflection as the "second act" of theology. We have noted, for example, Gutiérrez's contention that the "organic intellectual" has an important role to fulfill in balancing the first and second acts of theology. Liberation theologians shy away from any hint of a dualism that separates the knower from the doer; they are wary of armchair theologians who spin out their theories of dogma and the "ways of God" apart from the scramble of the rea! world. For this reason they disdain the title "professional theologian," preferring to consider themselves Christian reformers working side by side with the poor and oppressed.

Certainly the liberation theologians make a valid point when they say that some theological models have been excessively theoretical and speculative. Moreover, it is important to remember that for them idolatry is a far greater enemy than is atheism. In Latin America, with its predominantly Catholic population, the problem is not belief in God, but belief in *whose* God. In Asia too, with its diverse religions, the problem is similar. Hence, the crux of the matter *is* a "battle of the gods"—whether God is with oppressors or with the oppressed. For this reason liberation theologians are less concerned with intellectual formulations and more concerned with the biblical demands of justice and love for the poor and oppressed.

One must also recognize, however, the critics' valid concerns. In their focus upon the need to make theology praxis-oriented and reflective of the conditions of the poor and oppressed, liberation theologians sometimes overlook or dismiss the intellectual nourishment that led them to their present convictions. To caricature all hard-nosed theological reflection as artificial and academic is to pave the way for all kinds of superstitious nonsense and self-pleading. Along this line one may rightly fault certain Third World liberation theologians for their wholesale condemnations of First World theology as out of touch with the real world. A case in point is José Comblin's contention that "any Latin American who has studied in Europe has to undergo detoxification before he begins to act." After all, First World theology shows as much variety as does Third World theology. Asian and African theologians might just as easily insist that anyone who studies in Latin America these days will have to be decontaminated before returning home. Such charges only distort the picture and impede genuine dialogue.

The role and significance of the transcendent remains a troubling issue for liberation theologians. Although appreciating their genuine concerns over idolatry, the question must still be raised, vis-à-vis some forms of liberation theology, Where is God in all this? What has happened to the Lord of history? Is eschatology strictly a human enterprise? For example, as we have seen, Rubem Alves accentuates the human and immanent so strongly in his later writings that he sounds like a secular humanist.

It is important for liberation theologians that the immanent and transcendent be understood as part of the same process. The crucial problem here is to find the kind of language that will not suggest a "two-realm" theory of reality yet will still allow for a sense of divine sovereignty and mystery in the larger scheme of things. Liberation theologians refuse to interpret the eschatological dimension as primarily transhistorical, for the only history we humans know is the history of our present existence. One cannot be saved apart from this historical condition.

We do not have precise language to allow for both immanence and transcendence without one being swallowed up by the other. Earlier in this century

Maurice Blondel attempted to resolve this dilemma by rejecting extrinsicism and affirming God's redemptive presence in human history. Gregory Baum has devoted considerable attention to the development of this "Blondelian shift," contending that God is not the "over-against" of humankind; "every sentence about God can be translated into a declaration about human life."[8] Here transcendence is understood not as a metaphysical dimension of being "out there," but as a way of expressing human openness to the new and the mysterious. The future can be different from the past, a key tenet that the "theologians of hope" consider to be the eschatological promise. This notion of transcendence is also suggested by Korean minjung theologian Kyun Young-Hak:

> Transcendence is not movement into some metaphysical world out there or into "Spirit," but is deeply rooted in the historical experience of the human.[9]

One of the most important contributions of Third World liberation theologians is their criticism of the traditional view of transcendence and their insistence that a new vision of transcendence can and must emerge.

"A POLITICIZED FAITH"

Another widespread criticism of Third World liberation theology, implied in the preceding two criticisms, is the claim that liberation theology politicizes the Christian faith. In the words of Bonaventure Kloppenburg:

> [Liberation theology tends to] reduce Christianity to a humanism pure and simple or a simple declaration of human rights, or a violent protest against the injustices wrought by those in power, or a mere critical reflection on the political order.[10]

There is no doubt that most Latin American and South African liberation theologians have affirmed again and again how essential it is for Christians to become involved in the political process, insisting that this is where authentic faith must be lived out. In their underscoring of this imperative, however, one sometimes gets the impression that, for these theologians, other dimensions of the Christian faith and other forms of liberation are less important. Consequently, critics charge liberation theologians with identifying liberation exclusively with freedom from political, social, and economic oppression.

There are three responses that must be made to this accusation. First, Third World liberation theologians are deeply distressed by the apparent indifference of church members—church officials in particular—to the suffering of the poor and oppressed, and their tendency to view the church as a kind of spiritual cocoon. Consequently, liberation theologians hammer away at the importance of political involvement if the concerns of the poor are to be taken seriously.

Latin American and South African theologians are particularly adamant on this point.

Secondly, although these theologians emphasize political involvement, this does not mean that they reduce the meaning of liberation to its political, economic, and social components. To make this accusation is to misread them. Gustavo Gutiérrez emphasizes the necessary spiritual component of liberation. Leonardo Boff contends that without prayer and meditation no liberation is truly Christian, and points to St. Francis as the true model for human liberation.[11] Ernesto Cardenal prefers the life of the Christian poet over the life of the Christian politician. J. B. Libânio points to "spiritual discernment" as an essential component of the political life. Rafael Avila weaves together the sacramental and political,[12] as does Tissa Balasuriya. The list could go on and on.

In addition, these theologians do not eliminate the devotional dimension of the Christian life, nor do they downplay personal sin. Most of them practice an intense prayer life as devout as that of any other group of theologians. It is true, however, that they come down hard on the social sins that cause massive human oppression. They will not budge one iota from their condemnation of social evils. But to conclude that this strong emphasis on the social dimension of the Christian faith is for them the be-all and end-all of their witness is to distort their views.

Thirdly, in their deep and abiding concern over social and political oppression, and in their equally heavy emphasis on the historical context, theologians of liberation have initiated a two-pronged thrust that will no doubt increase in intensity. Meanwhile, other "in-house" issues remain unresolved.

In general, Latin American liberation theologians focus on social and political oppression, South Africans on racism, and Asians on religious oppression. But all three groups have been seriously remiss in their failure to deal with sexism as a blatant form of oppression. In fact, in my survey of Third World liberation theology, I can only express dismay at the lack of sensitivity displayed by most Third World male liberation theologians to sexist oppression. Clearly these theologians need considerable conscientization in this area of liberation, and must become more aware of other forms of oppression that have eluded their liberation probe.[13]

Another vital issue is the difference in emphasis between most Latin American and South African liberation theologians on the one hand, and many African theologians outside South Africa on the other hand. Latin American liberation theologians have for the most part failed to appreciate their indigenous religions, whereas African theologians have taken great strides toward rediscovering their cultural and religious roots. James Cone is not alone in his contention that:

The extensive research that African theologians have done on indigenous African religions and unestablished forms of Christianity does not have its counterpart among Latin American liberation theologians.[14]

By the same token, not many African theologians outside South Africa have devoted sufficient attention to social issues. They contend, with John Pobee, for example, that racism is not a burning social issue in their countries. Here Third World liberation theology faces a crucial test. Liberation theologians must beware of becoming elitist by insisting on setting the agenda for all subsequent forms of liberation theology. A focus on economic, social, political, sexual, and racial oppression, *and* an appreciation for native religions and cultures, are both prerequisite for the development of a full-blown liberation theology. South Africans Desmond Tutu and Allan Boesak are correct in insisting that that these two ingredients of liberation theology must be seen as complementary and not mutually exclusive. Thus, an important model today for Third World liberation theology is minjung theology of South Korea, which zeroes in on both human oppression and its indigenous shamanistic roots.

A corollary to the problem of the relationship between Christianity and politics is the criticism that some forms of liberation theology encourage priests—especially in Latin America—to become involved in partisan politics if they are to fulfill their proper role as active agents for social change. Should priests be primarily spiritual leaders, or should they engage also in direct, even controversial, political action?

This is clearly a complex and controversial issue. Priests as human beings and as representatives of the church are obligated to be involved in the life of the world. The church and its priests cannot and should not exist apart from the world they are called to serve. (In chapter 1, above, it was noted that Latin American priests have had a long tradition of involvement in politics—on the side of oppressors!) But how extensive should such political involvement be? How can priests work for social justice today if they live in a spiritual hermitage? By remaining aloof, they are by default lining up on the side of oppressors.

What complicates the issue even further is that the church aggressively encourages priests to become personally involved in combatting certain evils. For example, the Catholic Church, in the person of Pope John Paul II, takes a strong public stand against abortion. But are genocide, torture, or murder by starvation and poverty any less evil than abortion? The Catholic Church puts and keeps itself in a highly ambivalent position when it is so selective about which social issues deserve partisan involvement and which do not.

Liberation theologians differ among themselves as to the nature and extent of priestly and personal involvement in partisan social issues. But they do agree that it should be a major concern of theology to show preference for the poor and to seek to change the structures of society that keep the oppressed in substandard living conditions. Yet, at the same time, some proponents of a politically engaged church must beware of becoming uncritical advocates of "people's churches" working outside the institutional church and sometimes dogmatically claiming to know how the wrongs of the world can be righted. These "people's churches" have an important role to perform, but they are also not without blemish. Phillip Berryman correctly warns:

> The possibility of a revolution becoming a new oppression is not utterly discounted (even though the stress here has been on a critical support for the revolution). Christians should be vigilant not only about that ultimate possibility, but also particular developments that could eventually turn out to be steps in that direction.[15]

But opponents of liberation theology render a disservice when they brand activist priests Marxists or communists. Columnist Jack Anderson's reference to some activist priests in Central America "who have developed a schoolboy crush on Marxist revolutionaries" only reflects his own naivety.[16]

"CHRISTIAN AND MARXIST?"

Another criticism leveled against Third World liberation theology is its tendency to link an understanding of Christianity with socialism or Marxism, and its disavowal of capitalism as a viable option. Kloppenburg maintains that, for Latin American liberation theologians, "one cannot be an authentic Christian and still adhere to an economic system of the liberal or capitalist type."[17]
Kloppenburg comments:

> The difficulty with some forms of the theology of liberation is not that they should have the Church become flesh in a socialist system; such an attempt, to the extent that it is genuinely compatible with the Gospel is, on the contrary, good and even necessary, wherever socialist systems are given as part of the situation. The real difficulty is rather the attempt to link the Church in an exclusive and indissoluble way with these systems, to the point of rejecting all others as incompatible with the Gospel message of liberation.[18]

There is no doubt that a definite preference for socialism and a strong opposition to capitalism are widespread among Third World liberation theologians, especially in Latin America. Gustavo Gutiérrez, José Míguez Bonino, Juan Segundo, Hugo Assmann, José Miranda, José Comblin, and most of their colleagues are in full agreement on this point. In Africa, Allan Boesak has expressed similar views, as have Tissa Balasuriya, Edicio de la Torre, and Geevarghese Mar Osthathios in Asia.

This is not really surprising. After all, as many observers agree—regardless of whether or not they are advocates of liberation theology—capitalism and its twin, colonialism (or neocolonialism), have caused many of the social inequalities found throughout the Third World. And when social inequalities become as blatant and extreme as they are in so many parts of the Third World, it seems only natural to blame the economic system that has nurtured this state of affairs.

But it is important to note that not one liberation theologian covered in this volume accepts socialism or Marxism "hook, line, and sinker." Most of them clearly prefer "the socialist way" to "the capitalist way," but always with qualification.

Gustavo Gutiérrez admits that, for him, socialism represents "the most fruitful and far-reaching approach, but socialism is not without its defects"; liberation must never be equated with any social system. Juan Segundo believes that a "sensibility of the left is an intrinsic feature of an authentic theology," but he is critical of Marxist ideology and insists that in his version of socialism ownership should be exercised in true communities, not in a "useless statism." Hugo Assmann faults Marxism for its over emphasis on economic factors. José Miranda, probably the most vigorous advocate of Marxism among the theologians we have covered, is highly critical of doctrinaire Marxism; for him, communism means controlling resources in a more equitable manner than does capitalism. José Míguez Bonino advocates a new form of socialism that seeks to eliminate the basic inequalities of the capitalist system without becoming a mere imitation of doctrinaire Marxism. José Comblin criticizes Marxism for its lack of freedom and its attempted expulsion of God from humankind and history. Enrique Dussel favors socialism over capitalism, but argues that socialism need not be Marxist, and he criticizes Marxism for failing to affirm the Other. Otto Maduro is an avowed Marxist who insists that Marxist social analysis must be radically reinterpreted for the Latin American context. Aldolfo Pérez Esquivel favors neither capitalism nor communism, but instead suggests a new form of socialism that would encourage "self-management and sharing." Allan Boesak and Hélder Câmara opt for a social democracy in which all adults would have the opportunity to take part in the decision-making process. Tissa Balasuriya is highly critical of the profit motive behind capitalism and suggests a form of socialism in which there would be common ownership of the means of production and distribution. He also believes that Christians and Marxists have much to teach one another. Mar Osthathios believes that Christianity is easier to practice in a socialist than in a capitalist society, but he has many objections to communism.

Third World liberation theologians clearly are not of one mind in their approach to socialism-Marxism-communism. Those who do favor it over capitalism do so with their eyes open to the defects of both doctrinaire socialism-Marxism-communism and their present manifestations in such countries as China and the Soviet Union.

The whole issue would be greatly simplified if there were common agreement on the meaning of the terms "capitalism," "socialism," "Marxism," and "communism." If, for example, Marxism meant (1) state ownership and complete state control of the economy, (2) the overthrow of nonsocialist governments by force, and (3) an atheistic worldview, then one would be hard put to single out any Third World liberation theologian discussed in this book who would qualify as a Marxist. If capitalism meant completely free enterprise based on privatism (no state ownership or control of the economy), is there any country today that would qualify as capitalist? Of course, these definitions of

Marxism and capitalism are of limited value. A Marxist, for example, can be a Christian, a Buddhist, an agnostic, or an atheist—so can a capitalist. If anyone who sees (class) struggle between oppressors and oppressed as the basic cause of social and economic inequalities may be labeled a Marxist, then surely every corporation and every academic community has a Marxist component: they witness a continual struggle to overcome inequalities between the different levels of management and labor; or, in the case of the academic community, between the administration and faculty, the tenured and nontenured, and so on. To participate in an ongoing class struggle to overcome social and economic inequalities does not necessarily make one a disciple of Karl Marx. Rather, for Third World liberation theologians, it means that one is a disciple of Jesus Christ.

If a Marxist is defined as a follower of Karl Marx, one must then ask: the early Marx, the later Marx, or the Marxist ideas espoused by one of his interpreters?

What these terms mean and whether they are used pejoratively really depends upon definers and users. Words such as "Marxism" and "socialism" can so easily become red flags of denunciation rather than vehicles of concepts useful for clarification. In March 1983, Bernard Sanders, the Socialist mayor of Burlington, Vermont, was reelected by a clear majority. When he was asked what he meant by socialism, he responded:

> We shouldn't live in a society where some people have huge amounts of wealth and power and other people have none.[19]

This in essence is what the Third World liberation theologians are saying. And it is misleading—if not also dishonest—to wave a red flag and brand them and Mayor Sanders Marxists.[20]

It would be equally unfair to label Joseph Ramos, an ardent critic of liberation theology, a socialist merely because he too believes in a more equitable distribution of property, power, and opportunities in the Third World. Ramos contends that the basic problem for Latin America lies not in private property as such, but in its concentration in the hands of a few. Ramos argues that economic dependence itself does not limit Latin American development any more than, for example, U. S. investment in the Japanese economy limits its development. The basic problem, he believes, is distribution, not dependence or development. Ramos admits the existence of class struggle in Latin America, but he believes it naive to think that such struggles will end through the elimination of private property. After all, "oppression and domination are not peculiar to the system of private property."[21] According to Ramos, Latin America could improve its economic status by importing more capital, thus creating a higher degree of productivity, more jobs, and better distribution. He concludes:

> Economic development and the elimination of poverty do not depend so much on what others do for us, but on what we do for ourselves. Despite

our dependency, we have a sufficient degree of freedom to eliminate these problems and policies within our reach.[22]

Ramos's views are important in challenging the economic "dependency and development" assumptions held by many Latin American theologians. His advocacy of a more just distribution of property, power, and opportunities could lead to a more fruitful exchange between open-minded capitalists and socialists.

It is Joseph Ramos whom Michael Novak quotes extensively in his indictment of liberation theology in *The Spirit of Democratic Capitalism,* a book whose main goal is to orchestrate the "twilight of socialism."[23] Novak notes the "exceedingly flexible and experimental"[24] nature of democratic capitalism, asserting that it is not to be identified with "corporatism."[25] Yet, curiously, when Irving Howe suggests a more flexible view of socialism, one that would include democratic ideals and the abolition of poverty, but not the nationalization of industry, Novak accuses Howe of "serious acts of revisionism, which he [Howe] attempts to disguise with ideologically freighted words."[26] Novak even contends that:

Insofar as democratic socialism has given up the classic position of Marxism and the collectivized state, it may now be no more than a left-wing variant of democratic capitalism.[27]

If one accepts this argument, then one could say that insofar as democratic capitalism has given up the classic position of the privatized state, it may now be no more than a right-wing variant of democratic socialism. Novak may be correct in suggesting that some contemporary versions of socialism are difficult to distinguish from some views of democratic capitalism. What he fails to note, is that some contemporary versions of capitalism are equally difficult to distinguish from some views of democratic socialism.

Novak also points out that the economic and political system of the United States should not be identified with the kingdom of God. By the same token Third World liberation theologians would be the first to admit that the economic and political systems of the U.S.S.R., China, and Cuba should in no way be equated with the ideal socialist society.

What is especially disappointing about Michael Novak's criticism of Third World liberation theology and its alleged Marxist bias is that he has apparently done so little reading in primary sources on the subject. One finds in his writings no references at all to African and Asian liberation theology, and his references to Latin American liberation theologians are extremely cursory and selective. Equally disconcerting are some of his highly prejudicial and undocumented statements. For example:

The rich are useful because their odd tastes prevent our architecture from being monotonously bureaucratic. Their taste in hotels makes it possible for millions to stay, at least once or twice, in something other than middle-period Holiday Inn.[28]

Traditional Catholic ignorance about modern economics may, in fact, have more to do with the poverty of Latin America than any other single factor. . . .

One attraction of socialism may also be that it provides an excuse. Confronting the relatively inferior economic performance of their continent, the Catholic bishops of Latin America do not now blame themselves for the teachings about political economy which Latin American Catholicism has nourished for four hundred years. . . .

Conveniently, socialist theory allows them to blame the United States and other successful economic powers. No passion better fits the fundamental Marxist stencil, which offers a universally applicable paradigm: *If I am poor, my poverty is due to malevolent and powerful others.*[29]

In a subsequent article, "Liberation Theology in Practice," Novak continues to swing wildly. He claims, for example, that Gustavo Gutiérrez and Juan Luis Segundo do the "lion's share of the innovation" in liberation theology; "most of the rest is commentary." How can anyone who has done even a cursory reading of liberation theology make such a statement? Novak further charges that liberation theology "seeks intellectual prestige in posing as the voice of the poor," that it has not yet been shown that Latin America is "dependent" on the United States and multinational corporations, and that countries shaped by Confucian ideals have a better chance for social improvement than those shaped by Catholic social teaching.

Even more baseless is his accusation that liberation theologians are "speculative, ideological and academic," leveled in an essay in which Novak does not have a single footnote to substantiate any of his charges!

Let it be noted that most Latin American liberation theologians do not engage in specific analysis of the ills of their own particular society. In this sense Novak is correct in his charge that these theologians are more abstract than concrete in their social analysis. Their basic contention, however, is that Latin American dependence on other nations is the primary problem and that specific conditions will be corrected only if Latin Americans are encouraged to be independent, not subservient to foreign domination.[30]

In *Freedom with Justice: Catholic Social Thought and Liberal Institutions,* Novak argues that there is a direct relationship between the developing Catholic social tradition and liberal institutions:

Both traditions are centrally committed to the virtue of practical wisdom. Both hold that the perfect is the enemy of the good. Both are anti-utopian. Both recognize the frailties and weaknesses of human beings and the unpredictability of history [p. 17].

Novak exhibits his considerable analytical skills in discussing recent and contemporary social teachings, carefully referring to specific documents to substantiate his thesis. But it is important that Novak's book be read alongside Donal Dorr's *Option for the Poor: A Hundred Years of Vatican Social Teach-*

ing.[31] Unlike Novak, Dorr argues that these same Catholic social teachings betray an unambiguous "option for the poor." The odd point to underscore here is that the same Michael Novak who can be so scholarly and incisive in carefully documenting his partisan views on Catholic social teachings can be so unscholarly and opinionated when he discusses liberation theology.

James Schall, in his *Liberation Theology,* supports Novak's general position when he claims that as the virtues of capitalism are better appreciated, Latin America may well serve as a "spiritual last gasp for the validity of socialism and Marxism in our time."[32] Schall further argues that in Latin America today the poor are not getting poorer, but "everyone is getting richer" and that this success is due to the profit motive of capitalism.[33]

Perhaps the most innocuous critique of liberation theology to date is *Liberation Theology* edited by Ronald Nash (1984).[34] It consists of essays by ten prominent conservative thinkers. Most of these essays first appeared elsewhere and some of them much earlier; the Richard Neuhaus contribution was first published in 1973. Other than Gustavo Gutiérrez, who is blasted by virtually every author for his Marxist views, the only other Latin American liberation theologian in the entire book to be footnoted even once is Dom Hélder Câmara! Can this be called "scholarship"?

We should be able to get past the stage of waving red flags when it comes to the use of terms such as "capitalism," "socialism," and "Marxism." It is as unfair today to identify capitalism with an older rigid ideology as it is to identify socialism with Marxism. Marxism is a part of our history. We should be willing to incorporate some Marxist insights in the same way that we utilize the views of other thinkers from the past. As Juan Segundo has observed:

> There are problems connected with applying the label "Marxist" to a line of thought or a source of influence. First of all, those who identify themselves with Marx and his thinking have a thousand different ways of conceiving and interpreting "Marxist" thought. Aside from that fact, the point is that the great thinkers of history do not replace each other; rather, they complement and enrich each other. Philosophic thought would never be the same after Aristotle as it was before him. In that sense all Westerners who philosophize now are Aristotelian. After Marx, our way of conceiving and posing the problems of society will never be the same again. Whether everything Marx said is accepted or not, and in whatever way one may conceive his "essential" thinking, there can be no doubt that present-day social thought will be "Marxist" to some extent: that is, profoundly indebted to Marx. In that sense Latin American theology is certainly Marxist. I know my remark will be taken out of context, but one cannot go on trying to forestall every partisan or stupid misunderstanding forever.[35]

After reading all the criticisms of Latin American liberation theology for being Marxist-infested, one can only express surprise at the realization that it contains so few references to Karl Marx. Moreover, as already noted, positive references to Marx are laced with heavy doses of emendation. And, as also already noted, to point out social inequalities does not thereby make one a Marxist. To opt for the poor does not mean to opt for Marx. How can this be made clear to the critics?

One writer who understands these distinctions is Arthur F. McGovern, author of *Marxism: An American Christian Perspective.* In his fair and balanced treatment of this complex subject, McGovern explains to his readers:

> [This book] looks for what is positive in Marxist positions, agrees with much of the Marxist critique, disagrees with the Communist worldview and most Marxist-Leninist tactics, is cautious about easy solutions, and hence ends up more reformist than revolutionary, at least in respect to the United States.[36]

This is not the place to discuss McGovern's book at length, but the author's conclusion merits our attention:

> What can socialism contribute and what stance might a Christian take? If socialism cannot claim to have "the" solution, capitalism certainly does not. Socialism points to an important alternative possibility, and offers a needed critique of capitalism. For a Christian to work for a democratic socialism would seem a perfectly justifiable option. The very uncertainties about socialism might be all the more reason for Christians to be part of the movement to help shape its direction and values.[37]

Two other works related to this subject are worthy of mention here. In his perceptive book, *A Matter of Hope: A Theologian's Reflections on the Thought of Karl Marx,* Nicholas Lash points out the complexity of meanings that have been historically attached to both Christianity and Marxism: "Everything must be thought through once more: every term must sit for new examinations."[38] Although not a Marxist himself, Lash believes it quite possible that forms of Marxism could emerge that would be compatible with Christianity.

In another discriminating book, *Solidarity with Victims: Toward a Theology of Social Transformation,* Matthew Lamb stresses the crucial importance of a socially critical reconstruction of church beliefs and practices that would encourage solidarity with the poor and oppressed. Lamb does not deal directly with the relationship between Christianity and Marxism, but he bluntly maintains that "any economic system which intensifies poverty is not only immoral but also profoundly stupid."[39] Lamb's defense of the political dimension of all theology is an important point for both capitalists and socialists to bear in mind, as is his contention that political theology must be performed in "solidarity with victims."

Thomas Sanders, following the insights of Reinhold Niebuhr, protests the "moralistic ideology" of liberation theology. He faults liberation theologians for failing to recognize the ambiguity inherent in all social systems: one cannot easily separate socialists and capitalists, oppressed and oppressors, into the "good guys" and the "bad guys." Such an approach only leads to a naive "soft utopian" praise for the actions of socialist governments and an outright condemnation of capitalist systems. Sanders believes that liberation theologians could use a heavy dose of Niebuhrian realism.[40]

Dennis McCann picks up this Niebuhrian line of reasoning in his book *Christian Realism and Liberation Theology*:

> Is the meaning of Christianity immanent to history, or does it transcend history in any meaningful way? After wrestling with this issue for a number of years, I conclude that Niebuhr's "paradoxical vision" of the Hidden God's relationship to human history is a more adequate basis for practical theology and Christian social action than the vision of Christ the Liberator proclaimed by Latin Americans like Gustavo Gutiérrez.
> . . . North American theologians and social activists should not respond to this dispute by abandoning the legacy of Reinhold Niebuhr for the false promise of liberation theology. Instead, we should take liberation theology as a sincere but confused protest, a call to conscience that challenges us to rethink the theory and practice of Christian realism in light of the problems that await us in the 1980s.[41]

McCann's book includes a careful analysis of Reinhold Niebuhr's political views, along with his adoption and subsequent repudiation of Marxist theory. McCann sees many similarities between Christian realism and liberation theology. Both emerged as responses to major social changes that accompanied the forces of modernization and industrialization, both came out of the particular context of grass-roots pastoral ministry, and both seek to identify God's action in history and the proper human response. But the two approaches differ radically in what the proper human response should be. Liberation theologians emphasize class conflict and the need for a militant socialism in solidarity with the poor and oppressed. In McCann's words:

> Niebuhr moved toward the problematic of theological anthropology. By contrast, liberation theologians interpret God's action by identifying it with the historic aspirations of a particular group of human agents, the oppressed.[42]

For McCann, the basic issue separating Christian realism and liberation theology is one that I treated earlier: the role and meaning of religious transcendence in political action:

> If religious transcendence in its Christian form is indistinguishable from the revolutionary enthusiasm promoted by liberation theology, then in

principle there is not a conflict between Christianity and the dialectical vision, and the problem of politicization is meaningless. But if religious transcendence in its Christian forms is distinguishable as a spirit of disinterestedness, a heightened sense of humility born of faith, hope, and love, as Niebuhr experienced it in his paradoxical vision, then in principle there is a conflict between these theologies regarding the substantive meaning of Christianity for politics, and the problem of politicization is a serious one for practical theology.[43]

McCann's book is required reading for a careful analysis of the criticisms that have been made thus far of liberation theology.

Walter Benjamin faults Latin American liberation theology for its "ethical astigmatism" in failing to point out the evils of socialism so blatant in eastern Europe and the Soviet Union: "there is bondage elsewhere than south of the border."[44] Indeed this is true. But the problem in Latin America has been with capitalism. As socialist governments emerge in Latin America—in Cuba and Nicaragua, for example—and in other parts of the Third World, it will be vitally important for liberation theologians to be evenhanded in condemning the defects of socialism as well.

Jonathan Kwitney has given an additional reason why Marxist analysis has become important for Latin American liberation theologians, and why Soviet influence may be increasing in Latin America:

> There is only one reason why a country would want to adopt Marxism-socialism today. Unfortunately it is often a valid reason. Marxism-socialism is often the only way a country can avoid American imperialism. . . . Joining the Soviet arms network is often the only way to have a national government that is independent of CIA manipulation, and thus stand a chance of bargaining at arm's length with the multinational corporations.[45]

"IN FAVOR OF VIOLENCE"

A final major criticism of Third World liberation theology is that it advocates violence. Some of the rhetoric that certain liberation theologians occasionally use—oppressive social structures must be destroyed, the class system must be eliminated, the oppressor must be defeated, and the like—gives the impression that violence is endemic to liberation theology.

It is important to examine the meaning of the term "violence." For liberation theologians, violence is not only the use of physical power to achieve one's objectives. Violence is essentially the use of power to achieve one's own ends at the expense of others, whether an individual, a group, or a country. Violence is the aggressive tendency to dehumanize, the attempt to assert one's own will and power over others and the environment. From this perspective, poverty, political suppression, exploitation of the environment, economic subjugation, racism, and, one must add, sexism, are all forms of violence. In short, *violence is dehumanization and exploitation*. What Paulo Freire says of oppression might also be applied to violence:

> Any situation in which "A" objectively exploits "B" or hinders his pursuit of self-affirmation as a responsible person is one of oppression.[46]

Liberation theologians insist that violence is inherent in an unjust society. Oppressors are far more violent in using their almost unlimited power to suppress and exploit the oppressed than are the oppressed in seeking to rid themselves of dehumanization by means of the extremely limited power available to them.

It is for this very reason that the bishops at Medellín spoke of "institutionalized violence," an insidious kind of violence built into the very structure of Latin American society. Little wonder, then, that the bishops could appreciate the "temptation to violence" surfacing among the oppressed in Latin America:

> One should not abuse the patience of a people that for years has borne a situation that would not be acceptable to anyone with any degree of awareness of human rights.[47]

Violence has many faces. To accuse some liberation theologians of fomenting physical violence in some situations, without at the same time condemning those in power who continue to use violence, is hypocrisy of the worst kind. For, if those in power had as their primary concern the humanization of the social order, there would be no need for the powerless ever to respond with physical force. They would no longer be powerless. The crucial point, then, is that the poor, in their desire for human dignity, do not introduce violence into society; society is already riddled with violence. Therefore, we should not condemn some liberation theologians for condoning physical violence unless we first condemn the violence of those who make it necessary.

As a matter of fact, I find very little advocacy of violence on the part of Third World liberation theologians. José Míguez Bonino does declare that the violence of oppressors sometimes demands violence in return. José Comblin does not exactly advocate violence, but he points out that there are times when one faces an unavoidable option: no action, which only condones an oppressor's continuance of violence, or action that runs the risk of violence. Pablo Richard believes that violence is inevitable and notes that the book of Exodus is itself a book of violence. Leonardo Boff urges that the oppressed should use violence only when forced by oppressors to do so. All this seems entirely consistent with the Catholic theory of the just war, which condones war only if certain conditions are met, and even then only as a last resort. Liberation theologians' views concerning the use of violence seem tame in comparison with the statement in the United States Declaration of Independence, which affirms that all persons are created equal and have certain inalienable rights, including:

> Whenever one Form of Government becomes destructive of these ends, it is the Right of the People to alter or abolish it, and to institute a new Government.

Postscript

In his pioneering study, *The Coming of the Third Church*, Walbert Bühlmann points out that by the year 2000 the Western-oriented Christian church will be a minority. The center of membership and power, he writes, will have shifted from the First and Second Worlds to the Third. As a result, we Christians living in the more affluent nations will come to realize that "our air of superiority was certainly not according to Christ's will."[1] Bühlmann pleads for a "unity in pluriformity" approach, in which the church of the future will become increasingly more open to other manifestations and expressions of truth in the building of a new, worldwide social order based on justice. In their concerns for the liberation of the oppressed, all liberation theologians must keep in mind Bühlmann's vision of the church of the future.

What will this vision entail for Third World liberation theology? Let me cite here the insights of three Asian liberation theologians. The first comes from Indonesian theologian Albert Widjaja, who, as detailed in chapter 4, above, distinguishes between "theological begging" and "beggarly theology." The first phrase suggests the old practice of imitating and borrowing from established Western theologies, an approach that is no longer possible. The second phrase suggests an identification with social outcasts—in short, a "preference for the poor"—in the context of given local situations. For if we do not respond to the needs of the poor, we are not responding to Christ. At this point all forms of liberation theology are in full agreement and face their greatest challenge.

A second crucial insight comes from Choan-Seng Song who focuses on the image of the "third eye" in seeking to open up a vision of life that will enable us to see ourselves and others as we truly are. This image of the third eye—one might call it the indwelling of the Spirit—should enable us to see all of humanity as part of one family of God. All persons, using the lens most suitable to their particular historical setting, can focus on every other person as a full-fledged member of God's one family.

A final insight comes from Sri Lankan theologian Tissa Balasuriya, who warns against versions of liberation theology that are parochial in their outlook. To be sure, Balasuriya admits, liberation theologies must be contextual, but not at the expense of "a higher, wider, and deeper level of sharing among all human beings":

This calls for a transformation of ourselves from within our innermost being to accept all others as sisters and brothers. Our growth to a

118

planetary dimension is an invitation to spiritual deepening, a purification from selfishness to a more universal communion in real life, to our own humanization. Insofar as we do so, we shall become more truly civilized, approach the ideals of the best in our religions and cultures, and pursue the deepest and best aspiration of every human heart and mind.[2]

Here, then, is a future agenda for liberation theology that seems clearly implicit in the theologians discussed in this book. Each form of liberation theology must be indigenous, focusing on a preference for the poor in ways most appropriate to its own local setting. The Spirit of God must be the indispensable frame of reference by which all persons are judged, a Spirit ignoring boundaries of sex, race, religion, culture, or social and economic status. Finally, liberation theologies must never become exclusive properties of any past or present political ideology, but must always be open and sensitive to fuller manifestations of humanity that will encompass God's global family. With this vision of God's all-embracing love, liberation theologies will continue to insist with one voice that no one can be truly liberated until everyone is liberated, that no one can have dignity in God's eyes until everyone has dignity.

Notes

CHAPTER ONE

1. *Cry of the People* (New York, Penguin, 1982), p. 10.
2. "The Church in Latin America: A Historical Survey," in Henry A. Landsberger, ed., *The Church and Social Change in Latin America* (University of Notre Dame Press, 1970), pp. 40, 43.
3. *A History of the Church in Latin America* (Grand Rapids, Eerdmans, 1981), p. 51.
4. *Decolonizing Theology: A Caribbean Perspective* (Maryknoll, N.Y., Orbis, 1981), p. 16.
5. J. Lloyd Mecham, *Church and State in Latin America* (University of North Carolina Press, 1966), p. 38.
6. In Landsberger, *Church and Social Change*, p. 102.
7. *National Catholic Reporter*, Dec. 17, 1982, pp. 10–11.
8. *Latin American Theology: Radical or Evangelical?* (Grand Rapids, Eerdmans, 1970), p. 17.
9. *Gaudium et Spes*, in Joseph Gremillion, ed., *The Gospel of Peace and Justice* (Maryknoll, N.Y., Orbis, 1976), p. 243.
10. Ibid., p. 267.
11. *Mater et Magistra*, in Gremillion, *The Gospel*, p. 161.
12. See ibid., p. 149.
13. *Populorum Progressio*, in Gremillion, *The Gospel*, p. 388.
14. Ibid., p. 390.
15. Ibid., p. 395.
16. Ibid., p. 396.
17. Ibid.
18. Ibid., p. 402.
19. Ibid., p. 413.
20. In Irving Louis Horowitz et al., eds., *Latin American Radicalism: A Documentary Report on Left and Nationalist Movements* (New York, Random House, 1969), p. 194.
21. *A History*, p. 131. For further amplification of U.S. involvement in Latin America, see Penny Lernoux, *Cry of the People* and *In Banks We Trust* (New York, Anchor-Doubleday, 1984). See also Phillip Berryman, *The Religious Roots of Rebellion* (Maryknoll, N.Y., Orbis, 1984).
22. *A History*, p. 147.
23. *National Catholic Reporter*, Dec. 11, 1982, p. 11.
24. *The Church in the Present-Day Transformation of Latin America in the Light of*

the Council: Second General Conference of Latin American Bishops (Washington, D.C., National Conference of Catholic Bishops, 3rd ed., 1979).

25. Ibid., p. 23.

26. Ibid., p. 175.

27. "Latin American Liberation Theology," in Sergio Torres and John Eagleson, eds., *Theology in the Americas* (Maryknoll, N.Y., Orbis, 1976), p. 26.

28. *Basic Ecclesial Communities: The Evangelization of the Poor* (Maryknoll, N.Y., Orbis, 1982), pp. 64, 67–68.

29. *Pedagogy of the Oppressed* (New York, Herder and Herder, 1972), pp. 33, 85.

30. Quoted in Horowitz, *Latin American Radicalism*, pp. 492, 620. See also Jay Cantor, *The Death of Che Guevara* (New York, Knopf, 1983).

31. Quoted in Robert McAfee Brown, *Theology in a New Key* (Philadelphia, Westminster, 1978), p. 93. See also John Gerassi, ed., *Revolutionary Priest: The Complete Writings and Messages of Camilo Torres* (New York, Vintage, 1971).

32. Quoted in Landsberger, *Church and Social Change*, p. 151.

33. Câmara, *The Desert is Fertile* (Maryknoll, N.Y., Orbis, 1974), p. 16. See also Mary Hall, *The Spirituality of Dom Hélder Câmara* (Maryknoll, N.Y., Orbis, 1980). Another individual of immense importance is the martyred archbishop of San Salvador, Oscar Romero, who was murdered while celebrating Mass in March 1980. See Plácido Erdozaín, *Archbishop Romero: Martyr of Salvador* (Maryknoll, N.Y., Orbis, 1980); James R. Brockman, *The World Remains: A Life of Oscar Romero* (Maryknoll, N.Y., Orbis, 1982); *The Church is All of You: Thoughts of Archbishop Oscar Romero* (Minneapolis, Winston, 1984).

34. For the story of this movement, see John Eagleson, ed., *Christians and Socialism: Documentation of the Christians for Socialism Movement in Latin America* (Maryknoll, N.Y., Orbis, 1975).

35. Ibid., p. 4.

36. Ibid., pp. 161, 163, 168, 169.

CHAPTER TWO

1. *A History of the Church in Latin America* (Grand Rapids, Eerdmans, 1981), p. 112.

2. *A Theology of Liberation* (Maryknoll, N.Y., Orbis, 1973).

3. *A Theology*, p. 65.

4. *We Drink from Our Own Wells: The Spiritual Journey of a People* (Maryknoll, N.Y., Orbis, 1984). This significant book should be read as a sequel to his *A Theology of Liberation*.

5. "The Historical Power of the Poor," chap. 4 in Gutiérrez, *The Power of the Poor in History* (Maryknoll, N.Y., Orbis, 1983), p. 84.

6. *A Theology*, p. 90.

7. For further clarification of Gutiérrez's views on the relationship between Latin American liberation theology and recent European political theologies, see chap. 7, "Theology from the Underside of History," in his *The Power of the Poor in History*.

8. *A Theology*, p. 200.

9. "Liberation Praxis and Christian Faith," chap. 1 in Rosino Gibellini, ed., *Frontiers of Theology in Latin America* (Maryknoll, N.Y., Orbis, 1979), p. 28.

10. Gutiérrez has developed a "spirituality of liberation" in his *We Drink from Our Own Wells*.

11. *The Power of the Poor*, p. 100.

12. Ibid.

13. Anyone who has doubts on this point would do well to read his "Theology from the Underside of History" (see n. 7, above)—a brilliant analysis of theological and philosophical developments from the time of the Enlightenment and the French and American revolutions through the industrial and scientific revolutions to the modern period. Gutiérrez shows a profound grasp of those movements and the individuals— Kant, Hegel, Marx, Schleiermacher, Weber, Feuerbach, Maritain, Barth, Tillich, Bonhoeffer, and many others—who played major roles in them.

14. Cf. *The Power of the Poor*, p. 90.

15. *The Power of the Poor*, p. 66.

16. Gutiérrez, in Sergio Torres and John Eagleson, eds., *Theology in the Americas* (Maryknoll, N.Y., Orbis, 1976), p. 312.

17. Segundo, *The Community Called Church* (Maryknoll, N.Y., Orbis, 1973), p. 98.

18. *The Sacraments Today* (Maryknoll, N.Y., Orbis, 1974), p. 99.

19. *Our Idea of God* (Maryknoll, N.Y., Orbis, 1974), p. 4.

20. Ibid., p. 56.

21. Ibid., p. 182.

22. Maryknoll, N.Y., Orbis, 1976, p. 8.

23. Ibid., p. 27.

24. Ibid., p. 68.

25. "Capitalism Versus Socialism: Crux Theologica," in Rosino Gibellini, ed., *Frontiers of Theology in Latin America*, p. 257.

26. Ibid., p. 255.

27. "Social Justice and Revolution," *America*, April 27, 1968, p. 577.

28. Maryknoll, N.Y., Orbis, 1984, p. 142.

29. Ibid., p. 301.

30. An excellent book for gaining a greater appreciation of Segundo is Alfred T. Hennelly's *Theologies in Conflict: The Challenge of Juan Luis Segundo* (Maryknoll, N.Y., Orbis, 1979).

31. Alves was born in 1933. He teaches at the Campinas State University in Brazil.

32. *The Liberation of Theology*, p. 145.

33. *A Theology of Human Hope* (St. Meinard, Ind., Abbey Press, 1969), p. 67.

34. Ibid., p. 163.

35. Ibid., p. 99.

36. In Rosino Gibellini, ed., *Frontiers of Theology in Latin America*, chap. 13.

37. Quoted in Martin Marty and Dean Peerman, eds., *New Theology No. 9* (New York, Macmillan, 1972), p. 237.

38. "From Paradise to the Desert," pp. 290–91.

39. Ibid., p. 293.

40. Maryknoll, N.Y., Orbis, 1984, pp. 18, 90.

41. "Karl Barth and Liberation Theology," *The Journal of Religion*, vol. 63, no. 3, July 1983, p. 261.

42. Leonardo Boff, a Franciscan priest, was born in 1938. He studied theology and philosophy at Curitiba and Petrópolis in Brazil and later studied at Oxford, Louvain, Würzburg, and Munich, where he received his doctorate. He is professor of systematic theology at the Petrópolis Institute for Philosophy and Theology.

43. Maryknoll, N.Y., Orbis, 1978.

44. *Jesus Christ Liberator*, p. 63.

45. Ibid., p. 87.

46. Ibid., pp. 238–39.

47. Ibid., p. 250.

48. Ibid., p. 295.

49. Maryknoll, N.Y., Orbis, 1980, p. 126.

50. *Saint Francis: A Model for Human Liberation* (New York, Crossroad, 1982).

51. *The Lord's Prayer: The Prayer of Integral Liberation* (Maryknoll, N.Y., Orbis, 1983). Another splendid example of a "spirituality of liberation" is *Salvation and Liberation: In Search of a Balance Between Faith and Politics* (Maryknoll, N.Y., Orbis, 1984), which Boff co-wrote with his brother Clodovis. Boff's book *Ecclesiogenesis: The Base Communities Reinvent the Church* (Maryknoll, N.Y., Orbis, 1986), explores Brazil's basic Christian communities and illuminates Boff's contention that there are different "ways of being church." One of Boff's most original and controversial works is *Church: Charism and Power: Liberation Theology and the Institutional Church* (New York, Crossroad, 1985). In this volume, Boff presents the church, not as the City of God, 'mother teacher,' or sacrament of salvation, but rather as 'a church from the poor,' a church that insists that "without the preaching of justice there is no gospel of Jesus Christ." It is this book, with its critique of the hierarchical structure of the church, that prompted a Vatican statement in March of 1985 condemning certain of Boff's views.

52. Born in Brazil in 1933, Assmann studied sociology and philosophy in his native country, and studied theology in Rome. He has earned a doctorate in theology, a licentiate in the social sciences, and a special diploma in the study of the mass media. He has taught theology at Jesuit seminaries in São Leopoldo and Porto Alegre, and served as director of the Theological Institute in São Paulo.

53. Maryknoll, N.Y., Orbis, 1976.

54. Ibid., p. 56.

55. Ibid., p. 104.

56. "The Power of Christ in History: Conflicting Christologies and Discernment," in Gibellini, *Frontiers of Theology in Latin America*, p. 144.

57. Assmann, "The Faith of the Poor in Their Struggle with Idols," in Pablo Richard et al., *The Idols of Death and the God of Life* (Maryknoll, N.Y., Orbis, 1983), p. 228.

58. Miranda studied economics in Germany at the Universities of Munich and Münster and in 1967 received a licentiate in biblical science from the Biblical Institute, Rome. He teaches at the Universidad Metropolitan Tztapalapa in Mexico City.

59. Maryknoll, N.Y., Orbis, 1974.

60. *Marx and the Bible*, p. 277.

61. Maryknoll, N.Y., Orbis, 1977, p. 137.

62. *Being and the Messiah*, pp. 37–38.

63. Maryknoll, N.Y., Orbis, 1980, p. xi.

64. *Marx against the Marxists*, p. 61.

65. Ibid., p. 102.

66. Ibid., p. 123.

67. Maryknoll, N.Y., Orbis, 1982, pp. 1–2.

68. *Communism*, pp. 6–7.

69. Ibid., p. 69.

70. *The Militant Gospel: A Critical Introduction to Political Theologies* (Maryknoll, N.Y., Orbis, 1977), p. 374.

71. *A Matter of Hope: A Theologian's Reflections on the Thought of Karl Marx* (University of Notre Dame Press, 1981), p. 4.

72. *Marxism: An American Christian Perspective* (Maryknoll, N.Y., Orbis, 1980), p. 194.

73. Míguez Bonino was born in Argentina in 1924. He attended the Evangelical Theologate in Buenos Aires, as well as Emory University and Union Theological Seminary in the United States. Ordained to the Methodist ministry in 1948, he served churches in Argentina and Bolivia, and was an official observer of the United Methodist Church at Vatican II. Since 1954 he has been professor of systematic theology at the Higher Evangelical Institute for Theological Studies in Buenos Aires.

74. Philadelphia, Fortress, 1975.

75. Ibid., p. 119.

76. Ibid., p. 149. In his "An Open Letter to José Míguez Bonino," Jürgen Moltmann responds directly to Míguez Bonino's criticism, contending that Míguez Bonino and his Latin American colleagues are closer to European political theology than they care to admit and that in their use of the critical analysis of the European Karl Marx they are less distinctive than they think they are (*Christianity and Crisis*, March 29, 1976).

77. "Historical Praxis and Christian Identity," in Rosino Gibellini, ed., *Frontiers of Theology in Latin America*, p. 263.

78. Ibid., p. 272.

79. Grand Rapids, Eerdmans, 1976, p. 7.

80. In James Wall, ed., *Theologians in Transition* (New York, Crossroad, 1981), pp. 175–76.

81. Maryknoll, N.Y., Orbis, 1983.

82. Philadelphia, Fortress, 1983.

83. *Political Ethics*, p. 65.

84. Jon Sobrino was born in Spain, received a master's degree in engineering mechanics at St. Louis University in 1965 and a doctorate in theology from the Hochschule Sankt Georgen, Frankfurt, in 1975. He is professor of philosophy and theology at the Universidad José Simeón Cañas, San Salvador.

85. Maryknoll, N.Y., Orbis, 1978.

86. *Christology*, p. 337.

87. Ibid., p. 353.

88. Ibid., p. 368.

89. Ibid., p. 229.

90. In *Liberación y cautiverio* (Mexico City, 1976), pp. 177–207.

91. "Theological Understanding," p. 207.

92. "The Witness of the Church in Latin America," in Sergio Torres and John Eagleson, eds., *The Challenge of Basic Christian Communities* (Maryknoll, N.Y., Orbis, 1981), p. 181.

93. In Pablo Richard et al., *The Idols of Death and the God of Life: A Theology* (Maryknoll, N.Y., Orbis, 1983), chap. 4.

94. *Christian Realism and Liberation Theology: Practical Theologies in Creative Conflict* (Maryknoll, N.Y., Orbis, 1981), p. 221.

95. Quoted in Martin Lange and Reinhold Iblacker, eds., *Witnesses of Hope: The Persecution of Christians in Latin America* (Maryknoll, N.Y., Orbis, 1980), p. 153.

96. Born in Belgium, José Comblin has a doctorate in theology from the University of Louvain. Since 1958 he has lived in Latin America. For several years a member of the faculty at the Theological Institute in Recife, until his expulsion from Brazil in 1972,

Comblin divides his teaching duties between the University of Chile (Talca) and the Catholic University of Louvain.

97. Maryknoll, N.Y., Orbis, 1979.

98. *National Security State*, p. 220.

99. Maryknoll, N.Y., Orbis, 1979.

100. Maryknoll, N.Y., Orbis, 1976.

101. Maryknoll, N.Y., Orbis, 1977.

102. *The Meaning of Mission*, p. 60.

103. Quoted in Alfredo Fierro, *The Militant Gospel: A Critical Introduction to Political Theologies* (Maryknoll, N.Y., Orbis, 1977), p. 352.

104. Quoted in Alejandro Cussianovich, *Religious Life and the Poor* (Maryknoll, N.Y., Orbis, 1979), p. 14.

105. Born in Argentina, Dussel received his licentiate in philosophy from the University of Mendoza in Argentina, his Ph.D. in philosophy from the University of Madrid, a doctorate in history from the Sorbonne, and a licentiate in theology from the Catholic Institute of Paris. For several years he taught at Cuzo University in Mendoza until his activities in behalf of liberation forced him out of that post, and he teaches at the University of Mexico City.

106. *A History*, back cover.

107. Dussel, *Ethics and the Theology of Liberation* (Maryknoll, N.Y., Orbis, 1978), p. 162.

108. Enrique Dussel is one of the first Latin American liberation theologians to openly abjure ecclesiastical discrimination against women. He writes: "We feel confident that in the future we will see women priests, women bishops, and some day—and why not?—a woman pope. There is no theological or genetic objection: the woman is a human person" (*Ethics*, p. 113).

109. In Torres and Eagleson, *Theology in the Americas*, p. 290.

110. "The Kingdom of God and the Poor," *International Review of Missions*, April 1979, p. 115.

111. A native of Chile, Segundo Galilea lived for many years in Medellín, Colombia, where he directed the pastoral institute sponsored by the Latin American Episcopal Council (CELAM). He serves as a pastor in Santiago, Chile.

112. Maryknoll, N.Y., Orbis, 1981.

113. Maryknoll, N.Y., Orbis, 1982.

114. See Teófilo Cabestrero, *Ministers of God, Ministers of the People* (Maryknoll, N.Y., Orbis, 1983), pp. 13–43. Cardenal's *Flights of Victory/Vuelos de Victoria* (Maryknoll, N.Y., Orbis, 1985), a collection of poems composed after the fall of Anastasio Somoza in 1979, reveals why this priest-politician remains one of the foremost poets of Latin America.

115. A native of Venezuela, Peréz-Esclarín taught for several years at a university in Caracas and later left his academic post to live with the oppressed.

116. Maryknoll, N.Y., Orbis, 1978.

117. *Atheism*, pp. 57–58.

118. Maryknoll, N.Y., Orbis, 1980.

119. J. B. Libânio is professor of theology at the Pontifical Catholic University in Rio de Janeiro, Brazil.

120. Maryknoll, N.Y., Orbis, 1982.

121. José Severino Croatto is the first Catholic to teach at the Instituto Superior Evangélico de Estudios Teológicos (ISEDET) in Buenos Aires.

122. "Biblical Hermeneutics in the Theologies of Liberation," in Virginia Fabella and Sergio Torres, eds., *Irruption of the Third World: Challenge to Theology* (Maryknoll, N.Y., Orbis, 1983), p. 163.

123. "The Gods of Oppression," in Pablo Richard et al., *The Idols of Death and the God of Life*, p. 27.

124. Elsa Tamez is professor of biblical studies at the Seminario Bíblico Latinoamericano, San José, Costa Rica.

125. Maryknoll, N.Y., Orbis, 1982.

126. In Fabella and Torres, *Irruption of the Third World*, p. 186.

127. A native of Venezuela, Otto Maduro teaches philosophy at the University of the Andes in Merida, Venezuela.

128. Maryknoll, N.Y., Orbis, 1982.

129. *Social Conflicts*, p. 36.

130. Noel Leo Erskine is a member of the faculty of Candler School of Theology at Emory University, Atlanta, Georgia.

131. Maryknoll, N.Y., Orbis Books, 1981, p. 118, quoting Father Daniel P. Mulvey.

132. Beatriz Melano Couch is professor of theology at the Union Theological Seminary in Buenos Aires.

133. In Torres and Eagleson, *Theology in the Americas*, pp. 304–8.

134. Ibid., p. 376.

135. Maryknoll, N.Y., Orbis, 1983.

136. *God So Loved*, p. xi.

137. Ibid., p. xiii.

138. A native of Chile, Pablo Richard teaches at the National University of Costa Rica.

139. In Richard, et al., *The Idols of Death*, chap. 1.

140. "The Latin American Church, 1959–1978," *Cross Currents*, vol. 28, no. 1, p. 36.

141. A native of Argentina, Juan Carlos Scannone is professor of philosophy and theology at the Universidad del Salvador in Buenos Aires.

142. "Theology, Popular Culture, and Discernment," in Gibellini, *Frontiers of Theology in Latin America*, p. 228.

143. Ibid., p. 231.

144. Maryknoll, N.Y., Orbis, 1983.

145. *Christ in a Poncho*, p. 10.

146. Ibid., p. 34.

147. Ibid., p. 135.

148. Other leading Latin American liberation theologians include Clodovis Boff, professor of systematic theology, Petrópolis Institute for Philosophy and Theology, Brazil; Carlos Mesters, professor of biblical studies at the same institute; Gilberto Gorgulho, professor of biblical studies, archdiocese of São Paulo, Brazil; José Oscar Beozzo, on the Faculty of Theology, N. Sankora da Assunção, São Paulo, Brazil; Carlos Palacio, professor of theology, Pontifical Catholic University, Rio de Janeiro, Brazil; Ignacio Ellacuría, professor of philosophy at the Universidad Centroamericana José Simeón Cañas, San Salvador; Julio de Santa Ana, studies coordinator for the World Council of Churches; Raul Vidales, a member of the Bartolomé de Las Casas Research Center, Lima, Peru; Franz Hinkelammert, director of postgraduate economics at CSUGA-UNAH, Honduras; George V. Pixley, Seminario Bautista, Mexico City; and Sergio Torres, executive secretary of the Ecumenical Association of Third World

Theologians (EATWOT). One of the best overviews of the church and liberation theology in Latin America is Edward Cleary's *Crisis and Change: The Church in Latin America Today* (Maryknoll, N.Y., Orbis, 1985).

149. *National Catholic Reporter*, Dec. 17, 1982, pp. 10–11.

150. In Torres and Eagleson, *The Challenge of Basic Christian Communities*, pp. 93–94.

151. In John Eagleson and Philip Scharper, eds., *Puebla and Beyond* (Maryknoll, N.Y., Orbis, 1979), p. 12.

152. Ibid., p. 25.

153. Huntington, Ind., Our Sunday Visitor, 1977, pp. 39, 46.

154. "The Preparatory Document for Puebla: A Retreat from Commitment," in Gutiérrez, *The Power of the Poor*, p. 122.

155. A special issue of *Cross Currents* (vol. 28, no. 1, Spring 1978), entitled "Puebla: Moment of Decision for the Latin American Church," documents the opposition to the preparatory document.

156. *Christianity and Crisis*, Sept. 18, 1978, p. 211.

157. *Third General Conference of Latin American Bishops: Evangelization at Present and in the Future of Latin America, Conclusions* (Washington, D.C., National Conference of Catholic Bishops, 1979), p. 113.

158. Ibid., p. 114.

159. Ibid., p. 115.

160. *Christianity and Crisis*, March 19, 1979, p. 59.

161. Gary MacEoin and Nivita Riley, *Puebla: A Church Being Born* (New York, Paulist, 1980), p. 101.

162. In Eagleson and Scharper, *Puebla and Beyond*, p. 346.

163. "Liberation and the Poor: The Puebla Perspective," in Gutiérrez, *The Power of the Poor in History*, p. 152.

164. In Eagleson and Scharper, *Puebla and Beyond*, p. 302.

165. *The Ecumenist*, vol. 18, no. 1, Nov.–Dec. 1979, p. 4.

166. *National Catholic Reporter*, April 20, 1984.

167. The entire text of the Ratzinger document can be found in the *National Catholic Reporter*, Sept. 21, 1984, pp. 11–14.

168. *The Washington Post*, Sept. 23, 1984.

CHAPTER THREE

1. Sergio Torres and John Eagleson, eds., *The Challenge of Basic Christian Communities* (Maryknoll, N.Y., Orbis, 1981), p. 266.

2. Ibid., p. 258.

3. *Toward an African Theology* (Nashville, Abingdon, 1979), p. 39.

4. Gwinyai Muzorewa, *The Origins and Development of African Theology* (Maryknoll, N.Y., Orbis, 1985), p. 55.
For a further discussion of the failure of African theologians outside South Africa to become involved in political, social, and economic issues, see Ephraim Radner, "African Politics and the Will to Silence," *The Christian Century*, vol. 101, no. 34, Nov. 7, 1984, pp. 1034–38.

5. Both terms are recent in origin. John Mbiti claims that the term "African theology" was first used in 1956. See P. D. Fueter, "Theological Education in Africa,"

International Review of Missions, 27 (Oct. 1956). Gwinyai Muzorewa suggests that the official beginning of African theology can be traced to the founding of the All African Council of Churches (AACC) in 1963.

6. For a discussion of this issue, see Muzorewa, *The Origins and Development of African Theology,* chap. 7. See also Justin S. Ukpong, "Current Theology: The Emergence of African Theologies," *Theological Studies,* vol. 45, no. 3 (Sept. 1984), pp. 501–36. Here Ukpong distinguishes three major theological trends that have emerged in Africa since the 1960s: African theology, South African black theology, and African liberation theology.

7. In Torres and Eagleson, *The Challenge of Basic Christian Communities,* p. 258.

8. *Perceptions of Apartheid: The Churches and Political Change in South Africa* (Scottdale, Pa., Herald, 1979), p. 11.

9. *Isolating Apartheid: Western Collaboration with South Africa* (Geneva, 1982), pp. 1, 11.

10. Marjorie Hope and James Young, *The South African Churches in a Revolutionary Situation* (Maryknoll, N.Y., Orbis, 1981), p. 84. The story of this pioneering institution is told in Peter Walshe, *Church versus State in South Africa: The Case of the Christian Institute* (Maryknoll, N.Y., Orbis, 1983).

11. London, Hurst, 1973.

12. *Black Theology,* p. 6.

13. Ibid., p. 61

14. Donald Woods, *Biko* (New York, Vintage, 1979), p. 79.

15. In Torres and Eagleson, *The Challenge of Basic Christian Communities,* p. 263.

16. John Webster, *Crying in the Wilderness* (Grand Rapids, Eerdmans, 1982), pp. 62, 64.

17. *Biko,* p. 421.

18. Ibid., p. 424.

19. Born in 1931, Tutu studied in England and was ordained an Anglican priest in 1961.

20. Webster, *Crying in the Wilderness,* p. 35.

21. Ibid., p. 42.

22. Ibid., pp. 49–50.

23. Allan Boesak did his graduate training at the Theological Seminary in Belville, South Africa, and Union Theological and Colgate-Rochester Seminaries in the United States. He received his doctorate in theology from the Theological Academy of Kampen in the Netherlands.

24. Maryknoll, N.Y., Orbis, 1977. See also his *Finger of God: Sermons on Faith and Socio-Political Responsibility* (Maryknoll, N.Y., Orbis, 1982).

25. *Farewell to Innocence,* p. 1.

26. Ibid., pp. 1–2.

27. Ibid., p. 42.

28. Ibid., pp. 148–49, 151.

29. Ibid., p. 7.

30. Maryknoll, N.Y., Orbis, 1984.

31. *Black and Reformed,* p. 95.

32. In Moore, *Black Theology: The South African Voice,* p. 34.

33. "Toward Indigenous Theology in South Africa," in Virginia Fabella and Sergio Torres, eds., *Irruption of the Third World* (Maryknoll, N.Y., Orbis, 1983), p. 69.

34. Ibid., p. 64.

35. "Some African Concepts of Christology," in G. F. Vicedom, ed., *Christ and the Younger Churches* (London, SPCK, 1972), pp. 51–52.

36. *Bantu Prophets in South Africa* (London, Lutterworth, 2nd ed., 1961), p. 281.

37. Harry Sawyerr, *Creative Evangelism: Toward a New Encounter With Africa* (London, Lutterworth, 1968).

38. Maryknoll, N.Y., Orbis, 1977.

39. Ibid., p. 41.

40. London, SPCK, 1970.

41. "Theological Impotence and the Universality of the Church," in Gerald Anderson and Thomas Stransky, eds., *Mission Trends No. 3: Third World Theologies* (New York, Paulist, 1976), pp. 6–19.

42. "The Biblical Basis for Present Trends in African Theology," in Kofi Appiah-Kubi and Sergio Torres, eds., *African Theology En Route* (Maryknoll, N.Y., Orbis, 1979), p. 89.

43. "An African Views American Black Theology," in Gayraud Wilmore and James Cone, eds., *Black Theology: A Documentary History, 1966–1979* (Maryknoll, N.Y., Orbis, 1979), p. 482.

44. Boesak, *Farewell to Innocence,* p. 143.

45. *The Christian Century,* Aug. 27–Sept. 3, 1980, p. 819.

46. "The Quest For an African Christian Theology," *The Ecumenical Review,* 27 (July 1975), p. 263.

47. "African Theology: Origin, Methodology and Content," *The Journal of Religious Thought,* vol. 32, Fall-Winter 1975, no. 2, p. 45. For further discussion of Dickson's views on a "theology of selfhood" and also his conviction that African theology should embrace both African cultural traditions *and* present-day socio-economic oppression, see his *Theology in Africa* (Maryknoll, N.Y., Orbis, 1984).

48. Maryknoll, N.Y., Orbis, 1983, pp. 243-44.

49. "The Value of African Religious Beliefs and Practices for Christian Theology," in Appiah-Kubi and Torres, *African Theology En Route,* p. 111.

50. "Reflections from a Third World Woman's Perspective: Women's Experience and Liberation Theologies," in Fabella and Torres, *Irruption of the Third World,* p. 254.

51. "Third World Theology—What Theology? What Third World?" in ibid., pp. 217–18. Other important African theologians include Rose Zoé-Obianga of Cameroun; Constance Baratang of South Africa; Gabriel Setiloane of Botswana; Ogbu Kalu of Nigeria; Kodwo Ankrah of Uganda; Bishop T. Tshibangu of Zaire; P. A. Kalilombe of Malawi; Nigundu Mushete of Zaire; Douglas Makhathini of South Africa.

52. *Polygamy Reconsidered: African Plural Marriage and the Christian Churches* (Maryknoll, N.Y., Orbis, 1975), p. 114.

53. *African Widows* (Maryknoll, N.Y., Orbis, 1979), p. 214.

54. The entire issue of *International Review of Missions,* vol. 64, no. 254 (April 1975), is devoted to the moratorium debate.

55. *Polygamy Reconsidered,* p. 60.

CHAPTER FOUR

1. There are important exceptions—e.g., the Orthodox churches.

2. See Hans-Ruedi Weber, *Asia and the Ecumenical Movement, 1895–1961* (London, SCM, 1966), p. 15.

3. Ibid., p. 197.

4. James M. Phillips, *From the Rising of the Sun* (Maryknoll, N.Y., Orbis, 1981), p. 228.

5. Kosuke Koyama has served as executive director of the Association of Theological Schools in South Asia, dean of the Southeast Asia Graduate School of Theology, and professor of Ecumenics and World Christianity at Union Theological Seminary in New York.

6. Maryknoll, N.Y., Orbis, 1974, pp. vii–viii.

7. *Waterbuffalo Theology,* p. 7.

8. Ibid., p. 83.

9. Ibid., p. 220.

10. *No Handle on the Cross* (Maryknoll, N.Y., Orbis, 1977), p. 33.

11. Ibid., p. 106.

12. Maryknoll, N.Y., Orbis, 1979.

13. *Three Mile An Hour God,* p. 6.

14. Ibid., p. 118. In his book *Mount Fuji and Mount Sinai: A Critique of Idols* (Maryknoll, N.Y., Orbis, 1985), Koyama relates his own spiritual pilgrimage, beginning with the experience of the devastation of Tokyo during the Second World War. He also provides his assessment of Japanese religious traditions and affirms the need for creative dialogue between Asian spirituality (Mount Fuji) and biblical spirituality (Mount Sinai).

15. In John C. England, ed., *Living Theology in Asia* (Maryknoll, N.Y., Orbis, 1982), p. 41.

16. Ibid., p. 46.

17. "Theological Reconstruction," in England, *Living Theology in Asia,* p. 64.

18. "Evangelism Today," in England, *Living Theology in Asia,* pp. 76–83.

19. Peter K. H. Lee, "Between the Old and the New," in Sergio Torres and Virginia Fabella, eds., *The Emergent Gospel* (Maryknoll, N.Y., Orbis, 1978), pp. 124–37.

20. Maryknoll, N.Y., Orbis, 1979.

21. *Third-Eye Theology,* p. 11.

22. Ibid., p. 119.

23. Ibid., p. 137. See also his *Theology from the Womb of Asia* (Maryknoll, N.Y., Orbis, forthcoming).

24. *Third-Eye Theology,* p. 200.

25. *The Compassionate God* (Maryknoll, N.Y., Orbis, 1982), p. xii.

26. Maryknoll, N.Y., Orbis, 1982.

27. Maryknoll, N.Y., Orbis, 1984.

28. "Liberation of People in History," *Southeast Journal of Theology,* 19, no. 2 (1978), p. 22.

29. Maryknoll, N.Y., Orbis, 1979.

30. *Eucharist and Human Liberation,* p. 82.

31. In Sergio Torres and John Eagleson, eds., *The Challenge of Basic Christian Communities* (Maryknoll, N.Y., Orbis, 1981), p. 261.

32. Ibid., p. 260.

33. "Toward the Liberation of Theology in Asia," in Virginia Fabella, ed., *Asia's Struggle for Full Humanity* (Maryknoll, N.Y., Orbis, 1980), p. 19.

34. Maryknoll, N.Y., Orbis, 1984.

35. *Planetary Theology,* p. 28.

36. Ibid., p. 95.

37. Ibid., p. 117.

38. See "Towards an Asian Theology of Liberation: Some Religio-Cultural Guidelines," in Fabella, *Asia's Struggle for Full Humanity,* pp. 75–96.

39. Other theologians from Sri Lanka who have also concentrated on developing a more positive relationship between Christianity and the religions of the East are Lakshan Wickremesingh, Anglican bishop of Kurunegala; Lynn de Silva, a member of the Ecumenical Institute for Study and Dialogue, Colombo; and D. Preman Niles, professor at the Theological College of Sri Lanka.

40. "The Filipino Christian: Guidelines for a Response to Marxism," in England, *Living Theology in Asia,* pp. 93–94.

41. "A Theological Perspective on Human Rights," in England, *Living Theology in Asia,* p. 109.

42. See *The Stones Will Cry Out* (Maryknoll, N.Y., Orbis, 1978).

43. "Faith and Life Reflections from the Grassroots in the Philippines," in Fabella, *Asia's Struggle for Full Humanity,* p. 138.

44. "Philippines: A Gospel for the New Filipino," in Gerald H. Anderson, ed., *Asian Voices in Christian Theology* (Maryknoll, N.Y., Orbis, 1976), p. 134.

45. "New Testament for a New Spirituality," in Emerito P. Nacpil and Douglas J. Elwood, eds., *The Human and the Holy: Asian Perspectives in Christian Theology* (Maryknoll, N.Y., Orbis, 1980).

46. "Some Prenotes to 'Doing Theology': Man, Society, and History in Asian Contexts," in Nacpil and Elwood, *The Human and the Holy,* p. 208.

47. Maryknoll, N.Y., Orbis, 1983.

48. *Ownership,* p. 155.

49. "The Justice of God," in England, *Living Theology in Asia,* pp. 219–20.

50. "Theological Priorities in India Today," in Virginia Fabella and Sergio Torres, eds., *Irruption of the Third World* (Maryknoll, N.Y., Orbis, 1983), p. 35.

51. "Socio-Economic and Political Reality in Asia," in Fabella, *Asia's Struggle for Full Humanity,* pp. 50–59.

52. "Orientation for an Asian Theology," in Fabella, *Asia's Struggle for Full Humanity,* pp. 108–23.

53. "The Church: The Bearer of Salvation," in England, *Living Theology in Asia,* p. 211.

54. *Theology of a Classless Society* (Maryknoll, N.Y., Orbis, 1980), p. 15.

55. Ibid., p. 53.

56. "A Methodological Approach to Third World Theology," in Fabella and Torres, *Irruption of the Third World,* p. 85.

57. "The Lordship of Jesus Christ and Religious Pluralism," in Gerald H. Anderson and Thomas F. Stransky, eds., *Christ's Lordship and Religious Pluralism* (Maryknoll, N.Y., Orbis, 1981), p. 42.

58. Other leading Indian theologians include D. S. Amalorpavadass, M. M. Thomas, and Ajit Roy.

59. Maryknoll, N.Y., Orbis, 1980.

60. *Compassionate and Free,* p. 5.

61. Ibid., p. 21.

62. Ibid., p. 150.

63. "Beggarly Theology," in England, *Living Theology in Asia,* pp. 154–55.

64. Ibid., p. 155.

65. "God's Suffering in Man's Struggle," in England, *Living Theology in Asia,* p. 18.

66. Ibid., p. 20.

67. Ibid.

68. "Messiah and Minjung: Discerning Messianic Politics over against Political Messianism," in the Commission on Theological Concerns of the Christian Conference of Asia, *Minjung Theology: People as the Subjects of History* (Maryknoll, N.Y., Orbis, 1983), p. 185.

69. "The Minjung (People) as the Subject of History," in England, *Living Theology in Asia,* p. 26.

70. See "Towards a Theology of Han," in *Minjung Theology,* pp. 55–69.

71. In 1975 Kim Chi-Ha was nominated for the Nobel Peace Prize.

72. *The Gold-Crowned Jesus and Other Writings* (Maryknoll, N.Y., Orbis, 1978), pp. 123–24.

73. Other leading Korean theologians active in the development of minjung theology include Suh Kwang-Sung David, formerly dean of Ewha Women's University, Seoul; Kyun Young-Hak, formerly professor of Christian Ethics, Ewha Women's University, Seoul; Ahn Byung-Mu, formerly director of the Theological Institute, Seoul; and Moon Hee-Suk Cyris, professor of the Old Testament, Presbyterian Theological Seminary, South Korea.

74. Other important Asian liberation theologians include Koson Srisang of Thailand; Khin Maung Din of Burma; Alan Saw U of Burma; James A. Veitch of Singapore; Vitalino R. Gorospe of the Philippines.

CHAPTER FIVE

1. *Temptations for the Theology of Liberation* (Chicago, Franciscan Herald Press, 1974), p. 2.

2. "Where Has Liberation Theology Gone Wrong?," *Christianity Today,* Oct. 19, 1979, p. 28.

3. *The Religious Roots of Rebellion* (Maryknoll, N.Y., Orbis, 1984), p. 277.

4. An example of using the Bible for one's own purposes can be found in Rosemary Ruether's *Sexism and God-Talk* (Boston, Beacon, 1983), where she argues that a proper feminist reading of the Bible would mean that "many aspects of the Bible are to be frankly set aside and rejected" (p. 23). This refreshingly candid assertion goes far beyond what most scholars would contend.

5. "Karl Barth and Liberation Theology," *Journal of Religion,* July 1983, p. 254.

6. Ibid.

7. *Faith and Freedom: Toward a Theology of Liberation* (Nashville, Abingdon, 1979).

8. *Man Becoming: God in Secular Experience* (New York, Seabury, 1972), pp. 23, 170, 181.

9. In *Minjung Theology,* p. 54 (see chap. 4, p. 68).

10. *Temptations,* p. 16.

11. For a fine example of a spirituality of liberation, see Leonardo and Clodovis Boff, *Salvation and Liberation* (see also chap. 2, n. 51).

12. *Worship and Politics* (Maryknoll, N.Y., Orbis, 1981).

13. Another major issue to which Third World liberation theologians have not given adequate attention is the world population explosion. From the mid-1950s to the mid-1980s, the world population nearly doubled: from 2.5 billion to almost 4.8 billion. Although it is expected to stabilize at around 11 billion by the year 2150, the largest

population increases in the intervening years will be in the poorer areas of the Third World. This can only mean that the gap between the rich and the poor will continue to widen. Third World liberation theologians of all religious persuasions dare not shirk their responsibilities to confront this controversial yet critical problem that has such staggering implications for the poor.

14. In Kofi Appiah-Kubi and Sergio Torres, eds., *African Theology En Route* (Maryknoll, N.Y., Orbis, 1979), p. 186.

15. *The Religious Roots of Rebellion*, p. 363.

16. *The Washington Post,* Jan. 22, 1984, sect. C, p. 7. In a similar display of unscholarliness, Paul Johnson, in a book of over 700 pages (*Modern Times: The World from the Twenties to the Eighties* [New York, Harper and Row, 1983]), dismisses Latin American liberation theology in one sentence, characterizing it as seeking "to transform Catholic action into a radical political force, operating from 'base communities' organized on the Communist cell principle and even advocating violence for the overthrow of oppressive governments of the Right" (p. 701).

17. *Temptations,* p. 24.

18. Ibid., p. 26.

19. *The Boston Globe,* March 2, 1983.

20. For a helpful clarification of the terms "communism," "socialism," and "Marxism," see Arthur F. McGovern, *Marxism: An American Christian Perspective* (Maryknoll, N.Y., Orbis, 1980), pp. 3–4. To illustrate the ambiguity of the term "Marxism," Paul Johnson insists that in essentials Lenin "was not a Marxist at all" (*Modern Times,* p. 54). Another helpful book that points out the different meanings of Marxism is: Wayne Stumme, ed., *Christians and the Many Faces of Marxism* (Minneapolis, Augsburg, 1984). Cornel West, in his *Prophesy Deliverance! An Afro-American Revolutionary Christianity* (Philadelphia, Westminster, 1982), argues that: "Stalinism is to Marxism what the Ku Klux Klan is to Christianity: a manipulation of the chief symbols yet diametrically opposed to the central values" (p. 136). West's thesis is that "in an alliance between prophetic Christianity and progressive Marxism—both castigated remnants within their own worlds—lies the hope of Western civilization" (p. 23). See also his "Black Theology and Marxist Thought," in Gayraud Wilmore and James Cone, *Black Theology: A Documentary History* (Maryknoll, N.Y., Orbis, 1979), pp. 552–67.

21. "Reflection on Gustavo Gutiérrez's Theology of Liberation," in Michael Novak, ed., *Liberation South, Liberation North* (Washington, D.C., American Enterprise Institute, 1981); see also "Dependency and Development: An Attempt to Clarify the Issues," ibid.

22. Ibid., p. 67. For a defense of neocolonialism and the role of the multinational corporations in Latin America, see Thomas Sowell, "Second Thoughts about the Third World," *Harper's,* Nov. 1983, vol. 267, no. 1602, pp. 34–42. An important article that analyzes the relationship of Latin America to Western political thought is: Michael Dodson, "Prophetic Politics and Political Theory in Latin America," *Polity,* Spring 1980, pp. 388–408.

23. New York, American Enterprise Institute/Simon and Schuster, 1982.

24. *Democratic Capitalism,* p. 334.

25. Ibid., p. 84.

26. Ibid., p. 208.

27. Ibid., p. 334.

28. Ibid., p. 213.

29. Ibid., pp. 272–73, 276.

30. See Michael Novak, "Liberation Theology in Practice," *Thought,* 64 (June 1984), pp. 136–49. This entire issue of *Thought* is devoted to "The Church in Latin America." Novak's article also appears as a chapter in his book *Freedom with Justice: Catholic Social Thought and Liberal Institutions* (New York, Harper and Row, 1984).

31. Maryknoll, N.Y., Orbis, 1983.

32. San Francisco, Ignatius Press, 1982, p. 89.

33. *Liberation Theology,* p. 171.

34. Milford, Mich., Mott Media, 1984.

35. *The Liberation of Theology* (Maryknoll, N.Y., Orbis, 1976), p. 35.

36. Maryknoll, N.Y., Orbis, 1980, p. 7.

37. *Marxism,* p. 323.

38. University of Notre Dame Press, 1982, p. 25.

39. New York, Crossroad, 1982, p. 5.

40. *Christianity and Crisis,* Sept. 17, 1973, p. 170. Rubem Alves in return has attacked Sanders's Christian realism as an American ideology having an "unambiguous relationship with colonialism, racism and economic exploitation" (ibid., p. 176).

41. Maryknoll, N.Y., Orbis, 1981, pp. 4–5.

42. *Christian Realism,* p. 154.

43. Ibid., p. 237.

44. "Liberation Theology: European Hopelessness Exposes the Latin Hoax," *Christianity Today,* March 5, 1982, pp. 21–23.

45. *Endless Enemies: The Making of an Unfriendly World* (New York: Cogdon & Weed), pp. 389–390.

46. *Pedagogy of the Oppressed* (New York, Seabury, 1970), p. 35.

47. *The Church in the Present-Day Transformation of Latin America,* p. 53 (see chap. 1, n. 24).

POSTSCRIPT

1. Maryknoll, N.Y., Orbis, 1977, p. 229.

2. *Planetary Theology* (Maryknoll, N.Y., Orbis, 1984), p. 95.

Select Bibliography

LATIN AMERICA

Alves, Rubem. *A Theology of Human Hope*. St. Meinard, Ind., Abbey Press, 1969.
———. *What is Religion?* Maryknoll, N.Y., Orbis, 1984.
Assmann, Hugo. *Theology for a Nomad Church*. Orbis, 1976.
Barreiro, Alvaro. *Basic Ecclesial Communities: The Evangelization of the Poor.* Orbis, 1982.
Berryman, Phillip. *The Religious Roots of Rebellion*. Orbis, 1984.
Boff, Leonardo. *Church: Charism and Power: Liberation Theology and the Institutional Church*. New York, Crossroad, 1985.
———. *Ecclesiogenesis: The Base Communities Reinvent the Church*. Orbis, 1986.
———. *Jesus Christ Liberator.* Orbis, 1978.
———. *The Lord's Prayer: The Prayer of Integral Liberation*. Maryknoll, N.Y./Melbourne, Orbis/Dove, 1983.
———. *Saint Francis: A Model for Human Liberation*. New York, Crossroad, 1982.
———. *Way of the Cross—Way of Justice*. Orbis, 1980.
———, and Boff, Clodovis. *Salvation and Liberation*. Orbis, 1984.
Brockman, James R. *The Word Remains: A Life of Oscar Romero*. Orbis, 1982.
———, ed. *The Church Is All of You: Thoughts of Archbishop Oscar Romero*. Minneapolis, Winston, 1984.
Brown, Robert McAfee. *Theology in a New Key*. Philadelphia, Westminster, 1978.
Câmara, Hélder. *The Desert is Fertile*. Orbis, 1974.
Cantor, Jay. *The Death of Che Guevara*. New York. Knopf, 1983.
Cardenal, Ernesto. *Flights of Victory/Vuelos de Victoria*. Orbis, 1985.
———. *The Gospel in Solentiname*. Orbis, 4 vols., 1976–82.
The Church in the Present-Day Transformation of Latin America in the Light of the Council: Second General Conference of Latin American Bishops. Washington, D.C., National Conference of Catholic Bishops, 3rd ed., 1979.
Cleary, Edward. *Crisis and Change: The Church in Latin America Today*. Orbis, 1985.
Comblin, José. *The Church and the National Security State*. Orbis, 1979.
———. *Jesus of Nazareth: Meditations on His Humanity*. Orbis, 1976.
———. *The Meaning of Mission: Jesus, Christians, and the Wayfaring Church*. Orbis, 1977.
———. *Sent from the Father: Meditations on the Fourth Gospel*. Orbis, 1979.
Dussel, Enrique. *Ethics and the Theology of Liberation*. Orbis, 1978.
———. *A History of the Church in Latin America*. Grand Rapids, Eerdmans, 1981.
Eagleson, John, ed. *Christians and Socialism: Documentation of the Christians for Socialism Movement in Latin America*. Orbis, 1975.
———, and Scharper, Philip, eds. *Puebla and Beyond: Documentation and Commentary*. Orbis, 1979.

Erdozaín, Plácido. *Archbishop Romero: Martyr of Salvador.* Orbis, 1980.

Erskine, Noel Leo. *Decolonizing Theology: A Caribbean Perspective.* Orbis, 1981.

Fierro, Alfredo. *The Militant Gospel: A Critical Introduction to Political Theologies.* Orbis, 1977.

Freire, Paulo. *Pedagogy of the Oppressed.* New York, Continuum, 1970.

Galilea, Segundo. *Following Jesus.* Orbis, 1981.

Gerassi, John, ed. *Revolutionary Priest: The Complete Writings and Messages of Camilo Torres.* New York, Vintage, 1971.

Gibellini, Rosino, ed. *Frontiers of Theology in Latin America.* Orbis, 1979.

Gutiérrez, Gustavo. *The Power of the Poor in History.* Orbis, 1983.

———. *A Theology of Liberation.* Orbis, 1973.

———. *We Drink from Our Own Wells.* Orbis, 1984.

Hall, Mary. *The Spirituality of Dom Hélder Câmara.* Orbis, 1980.

Hanks, Thomas D. *God So Loved the Third World: The Biblical Vocabulary of Oppression.* Orbis, 1983.

Hennelly, Alfred. *Theologies in Conflict: The Challenge of Juan Luis Segundo.* Orbis, 1979.

Horowitz, Irving Louis, de Castro, Josué, and Gerassi, John, eds. *Latin American Radicalism: A Documentary Report on Left and Nationalist Movements.* New York, Random House, 1969.

Hunsinger, George. "Karl Barth and Liberation Theology." *The Journal of Religion,* vol. 63, no. 3 (July 1983).

Landsberger, Henry A., ed. *The Church and Social Change in Latin America.* Notre Dame, Ind., University of Notre Dame Press, 1970.

Lange, Martin and Iblacker, Reinhold. *Witnesses of Hope: The Persecution of Christians in Latin America.* Orbis, 1980.

Lernoux, Penny. *In Banks We Trust.* New York, Anchor-Doubleday, 1984.

———. *Cry of the People.* New York, Penguin, 1982.

Libânio, J. B. *Spiritual Discernment and Politics: Guidelines for Religious Communities.* Orbis, 1982.

MacEoin, Gary and Riley, Nivita. *Puebla: A Church Being Born.* New York, Paulist, 1980.

Maduro, Otto. *Religion and Social Conflicts.* Orbis, 1982.

Mecham, J. Lloyd. *Church and State in Latin America: A History of Politicoecclesial Relations.* University of North Carolina Press, 1966.

Míguez Bonino, José. *Christians and Marxists: The Mutual Challenge to Revolution.* Grand Rapids, Eerdmans, 1976.

———. *Doing Theology in a Revolutionary Situation.* Philadelphia, Fortress, 1975.

———. *Toward a Christian Political Ethics.* Philadelphia, Fortress, 1983.

———, ed. *Faces of Jesus: Latin American Christologies.* Orbis, 1983.

Miranda, José Porfírio. *Being and the Messiah: The Message of St. John.* Orbis, 1977.

———. *Communism in the Bible.* Orbis, 1982.

———. *Marx and the Bible: A Critique of the Philosophy of Oppression.* Orbis, 1974.

———. *Marx against the Marxists.* Orbis, 1980.

Peréz-Esclárin. *Atheism and Liberation.* Orbis, 1978.

———. *Jesus of Gramoven.* Orbis, 1980.

Pérez Esquivel, Adolfo. *Christ in a Poncho: Witnesses to the Nonviolent Struggles in Latin America.* Orbis, 1983.

Richard, Pablo, et al. *The Idols of Death and the God of Life.* Orbis, 1983.

Segundo, Juan Luis. *The Community Called Church.* Orbis, 1973.

———. *Faith and Ideologies.* Orbis, 1984.

———. *Our Idea of God.* Orbis, 1974.

———. *The Liberation of Theology.* Orbis, 1976.

———. *The Sacraments Today.* Orbis, 1974.

Sobrino, Jon. *Christology at the Crossroads: A Latin American Approach.* Orbis, 1978.

Tamez, Elsa. *Bible of the Oppressed.* Orbis, 1982.

Third General Conference of Latin American Bishops. *Evangelization at Present and in the Future of Latin America: Conclusions.* Washington, D.C., National Conference of Catholic Bishops, 1979.

Torres, Sergio, and Eagleson, John, eds. *The Challenge of Basic Christian Communities.* Orbis, 1981.

———, eds. *Theology in the Americas.* Orbis, 1976.

AFRICA

Appiah-Kubi, Kofi, and Torres, Sergio, eds. *African Theology En Route.* Maryknoll, N.Y., Orbis, 1979.

Boesak, Allan. *Black and Reformed: Apartheid, Liberation, and the Calvinist Tradition.* Orbis, 1984.

———. *Farewell to Innocence: A Socio-Ethical Study on Black Theology and Power.* Orbis, 1977.

———. *The Finger of God: Sermons on Faith and Socio-Political Responsibility.* Orbis, 1982.

Dickson, Kwesi. *Theology in Africa.* Orbis, 1984.

Hillman, Eugene. *Polygamy Reconsidered: African Plural Marriages and the Christian Churches.* Orbis, 1975.

Hope, Marjorie, and Young, James. *The South African Churches in a Revolutionary Situation.* Orbis, 1981.

Kirwen, Michael. *African Widows.* Orbis, 1979.

Mbiti, John. *Concepts of God in Africa.* London, SPCK, 1970.

Moore, Basil, ed. *Black Theology: The South African Voice.* London, Hurst, 1973.

Muzorewa, Gwinyai. *The Origins and Development of African Theology.* Orbis, 1985.

Pobee, John. *Toward an African Theology.* Nashville, Abingdon, 1979.

Regehr, Ernie. *Perceptions of Apartheid: The Churches and Political Change in South Africa.* Scottdale, Pa., Herald, 1979.

Sanneh, Lamin. *West African Christianity: The Religious Impact.* Orbis, 1983.

Sawyerr, Harry. *Creative Evangelism: Toward a New Encounter with Africa.* London, Lutterworth, 1968.

Shorter, Aylward. *African Christian Theology: Adaptation or Incarnation?* Orbis, 1977.

Sjollema, Baldwin. *Isolating Apartheid: Western Collaboration with South Africa.* Geneva, 1982.

Sundkler, Bengt. *Bantu Prophets in South Africa.* London, Lutterworth, 2nd. ed., 1961.

Torres, Sergio, and Fabella, Virginia, eds. *The Emergent Gospel: Theology from the Underside of History.* Maryknoll, N.Y./London, Orbis/Chapman, 1978.

Tutu, Desmond. *Hope and Suffering: Sermons and Speeches.* Grand Rapids, Eerdmans, 1984.

Ukpong, Justin S. "Current Theology: The Emergence of African Theologies." *Theological Studies,* vol. 45, no. 3 (Sept. 1984), pp. 501–36.

Vicedom, G. F. *Christ and the Younger Churches.* London, SPCK, 1972.

Walshe, Peter. *Church versus State in South Africa: The Case of the Christian Institute.* Orbis, 1983.

Webster, John. *Crying in the Wilderness.* Grand Rapids, Eerdmans, 1982.

Woods, Donald. *Biko.* New York, Vintage, 1979.

ASIA

Anderson, Gerald H., ed. *Asian Voices in Christian Theology.* Maryknoll, N.Y., Orbis, 1976.

Avila, Charles. *Ownership: Early Christian Teaching.* Orbis, 1983.

Balasuriya, Tissa. *The Eucharist and Human Liberation.* Orbis, 1979.

———. *Planetary Theology.* Orbis, 1984.

Claver, Francis F. *The Stones Will Cry Out.* Orbis, 1978.

The Commission on Theological Concerns of the Christian Conference of Asia, ed. *Minjung Theology: People as the Subjects of History.* Orbis, 1983.

Digan, Parig. *Churches in Contestation: Asian Christian Social Protest.* Orbis, 1984.

England, John C., ed. *Living Theology in Asia.* Orbis, 1982.

Fabella, Virginia, ed. *Asia's Struggle for Full Humanity.* Orbis, 1980.

———, and Torres, Sergio, eds. *Irruption of the Third World.* Orbis, 1983.

Katoppo, Marianne. *Compassionate and Free: An Asian Woman's Theology.* Orbis, 1980.

Kim Chi Ha. *The Gold-Crowned Jesus and Other Writings.* Orbis, 1978.

Kitamori, Kazoh. *Theology of the Pain of God.* Richmond, Knox, 1965.

Koyama, Kosuke. *Mount Fuji and Mt. Sinai: A Critique of Idols.* Orbis, 1985.

———. *No Handle on the Cross.* Orbis, 1977.

———. *Three Mile an Hour God.* Orbis, 1979.

———. *Waterbuffalo Theology.* Orbis, 1974.

Nacpil, Emerito P., and Elwood, Douglas J., eds. *The Human and the Holy: Asian Perspectives in Christian Theology.* Orbis, 1980.

Osthathios, Geevarghese Mar. *Theology of a Classless Society.* Orbis, 1980.

Philips, James J. *From the Rising of the Sun.* Orbis, 1981.

Song, C. S. *The Compassionate God.* Orbis, 1982.

———. *The Tears of Lady Meng.* Orbis, 1982.

———. *Tell Us Our Names: Story Theology from an Asian Perspective.* Orbis, 1984.

———. *Third-Eye Theology.* Orbis, 1979.

Weber, Hans-Ruedi. *Asia and the Ecumenical Movement, 1895–1961.* London, SCM, 1966.

INTERPRETATIONS AND EVALUATIONS

Anderson, Gerald, and Stransky, Thomas, eds. *Mission Trends No. 3: Third World Theologies.* New York, Paulist, 1976.

Bühlmann, Walbert. *The Coming of the Third Church.* Maryknoll, N.Y., Orbis, 1977.

Dodson, Michael. "Prophetic Politics and Political Theory in Latin America." *Polity* (Spring 1980).

Dorr, Donal. *Option for the Poor: A Hundred Years of Vatican Social Teaching.* Orbis, 1983.

Ferm, Deane W. "South American Liberation Theology," in Ferm, *Contemporary American Theologies: A Critical Survey.* New York, Seabury, 1981.

Gonzáles, Juan Gutiérrez. *The New Liberation Gospel.* Chicago, Franciscan Herald Press, 1977.

Gremillion, Joseph, ed. *The Gospel of Peace and Justice.* Orbis, 1976.

Lamb, Matthew. *Solidarity with Victims: Toward a Theology of Social Transformation.* New York, Crossroad, 1982.

Lash, Nicholas. *A Matter of Hope: A Theologian's Reflections on the Thought of Karl Marx.* University of Notre Dame Press, 1981.

McCann, Dennis. *Christian Realism and Liberation Theology: Practical Theologies in Creative Conflict.* Orbis, 1981.

McGovern, Arthur M. *Marxism: An American Christian Perspective.* Orbis, 1980.

Ogden, Schubert. *Faith and Freedom: Toward a Theology of Liberation.* Nashville, Abingdon, 1979.

Shaull, Richard. *Heralds of a New Reformation: The Poor of South and North America.* Orbis, 1984.

Sowell, Thomas. "Second Thoughts about the Third World." *Harper's,* vol. 267, no. 1602 (Nov. 1983).

Stumme, Wayne, ed. *Christians and the Many Faces of Marxism.* Minneapolis, Augsburg, 1984.

West, Cornel, *Prophesy Deliverance! An Afro-American Revolutionary Christianity.* Philadelphia, Westminster, 1982.

Wilmore, Gayraud, and Cone, James, eds. *Black Theology: A Documentary History, 1966–1979.* Orbis, 1979.

Index

Compiled by James Sullivan

142